Theresa Clarke

GUIDING READERS

Making the Most of the 18 - minute Guided Reading Lesson

Lori Jamison Rog

Pembroke Publishers Limited

Pembroke Publishers
538 Hood Road
Markham, Ontario, Canada L3R 3K9
www.pembrokepublishers.com

Distributed in the U.S. by Stenhouse Publishers
480 Congress Street
Portland, ME 04101
www.stenhouse.com

We acknowledge the financial support of the Government of Canada through the Book Publishing Industry Development Program (BPIDP) for our publishing activities.

We acknowledge the assistance of the Government of Ontario through the Ontario Media Development Corporation's Ontario Book Initiative.

Library and Archives Canada Cataloguing in Publication

Rog, Lori,
    Guiding readers : making the most of the 18-minute guided reading lesson / Lori Jamison Rog.

Includes bibliographical references and index.
Issued also in electronic format.
ISBN 978-1-55138-273-9

    1. Guided reading. 2. Reading (Elementary) I. Title.

LB1050.377.R64 2012   372.41'62   C2011-907413-3

eBook format ISBN 978-1-55138-835-9

Editor: Kat Mototsune
Cover Design: John Zehethofer
Typesetting: Jay Tee Graphics Ltd.

Printed and bound in Canada
9 8 7 6 5 4 3 2 1

MIX
Paper from
responsible sources
FSC® C004071

Contents

Introduction

My husband and I, at our advanced ages, have decided to learn to speak Italian. One of the ways we practice is to read articles from *Corriere della Sera,* an Italian newspaper, while our teacher Filippo scaffolds us with word- and text-level support. Filippo knows to choose articles that are just beyond our reach: if the text is too hard, we won't have the strategies to cope with it; if the text is too easy, our understanding of the language won't increase.

Sometimes Filippo will choose a text that serves a specific purpose, such as an Italian translation of a Charlie Brown comic strip to practice the *congiutivo* verb tense. These lessons involve a little explicit teaching, a little modeling, and a whole lot of guided practice. We do the reading work while Filippo observes and intervenes as needed. To me, these lessons are what guided reading is all about: small, needs-based groupings; careful text selection; assessment-driven instruction; responsive teaching; and a delicate balance of success and challenge.

In 2003, I wrote a book called *Guided Reading Basics: Organizing, Managing and Implementing a Balanced Literacy Program in K–3,* which reflected what I had learned from early work on guided reading in my school division. These days, I travel across North America, working with schools and districts on best practices in reading and writing, and I believe that guided reading is more important than ever. But some of my thinking about guided reading has evolved in the past ten years.

Back then, if you dropped in on my guided reading lesson, you would likely see children reading quietly from individual texts while I listened to them, one by one, offering encouragement and occasional prompting. Today, you would still be likely to see children reading while I listen and guide. But you might also see children talking about strategies they have used, or engaged in interactive writing, or even playing games to practice specific skills. You are likely to see students reading leveled books, but you might also see them reading brochures, cartoons, websites, road signs, or recipes.

Ten years ago, my lesson preparation involved little more than selecting an appropriate text; my teaching was spontaneous and off the cuff, driven mainly by issues that arose from the students' reading. I still believe in the importance of that just-in-time teaching. But today, I rely on planning a little more and inspiration a little less. My lessons are more likely to be carefully structured around focus strategies and skills, with pre-determined pause points and discussion prompts, plenty of talk, and a range of guided practice routines.

In this book, I describe a model of guided reading instruction that is more intentional, prepared, and focused than the one I used a decade ago. I still want my students to learn to flexibly apply a range of processes to increasingly sophisticated text, but I now know that, on the journey to that independence, they may need to focus on specific reading strategies and processes. Today's guided reading is more purposefully aligned with the rest of the literacy program. For example, if I have been teaching the class about self-questioning during reading as part of my read-aloud, then I might have all my guided reading groups practicing "I wonders" with texts at their respective levels. And, while today's guided reading still emphasizes processing connected print, I might use part of the guided reading lesson to sort word cards or to build words with letter tiles—if that's what meets the needs of the group. Embedded into a global focus on making meaning from text are specific learning goals that I can teach, reinforce, and assess. This might mean using some of the guided reading session to play games with boards and dice to reinforce Kindergarteners' letter knowledge or explicitly teaching an advanced group of first-graders about a comprehension strategy that the rest of the class might not be ready for. It might mean pulling together a group of Grade 2 students who are at disparate reading levels but who all need to work on phrasing in oral reading. It might mean supporting students as they learn to read a website or travel brochure, even if it isn't technically at their "just-right" reading level.

I still believe that the structure of the guided reading lesson should be more about student reading and less about teacher talk. I still believe that students should be spending most of their time navigating connected text. I still believe in seizing the teachable moment. But in today's guided reading lesson, you'll see a lot more guided practice of specific strategies, much more talk about text, and a whole variety of literacy activities to meet student needs. Call it "guided reading" or call it "small-group instruction"—it's all about *guiding readers*. If we box ourselves into a narrow definition of guided reading, then we miss many of the opportunities that small-group instruction offers. The semantics don't matter, but the learning does. I have that small group in front of me with a precious 18-minute window in which to do what I can to help them become a little better at reading, writing, and thinking.

Why 18 minutes? That time frame initially arose out of a need to organize my literacy block into 20-minute segments. I would set a timer at 18 minutes to provide two minutes of transition time from one group to the next. As it turned out, 18 minutes was a serendipitous period of time. It is long enough for some sustained reading—by both the guided reading group and the independent learners—without depleting the limited attention spans of younger students.

Eighteen minutes is…the length of a coffee break (if you're not a teacher), the length of a sitcom without commercials, the length of time it takes to walk 1000 paces. The 18-minute time frame has received increasing attention recently with the renowned TED conferences, in which prominent thinkers and leaders in a variety of fields related to technology, entertainment, or design have 18 minutes to deliver speeches on their most important ideas. Again, why 18 minutes? Eighteen minutes is considered long enough to be serious, yet short enough to hold listeners' attention.

The 18-minute guided reading lesson may very well be the finest teaching we do. It provides that just-in-time teaching at the point of need, that opportunity to practice the habits of highly effective readers in a safe and supportive environment, that sensitive scaffolding that bridges readers from what they can do independently today to what they will be able to do tomorrow.

Eighteen minutes, however, isn't much time with a text. That's why I now plan for *sequences* of three or more guided reading lessons with each reading passage.

This extended experience with a text provides opportunities for rereading, discussing, working with print and language features, and elevating thinking.

For me, the greatest strength of guided reading is that it offers support for all the readers in our classrooms: the strongest and the weakest, the motivated and the indifferent, the million-word kids and the thousand-word kids. Even proficient readers—those who are already reading beyond grade-level expectations—need opportunities to extend their reach in literacy. We are dealing with a greater diversity of students in our classrooms than ever before. Guided reading enables us to support each one of them.

This book is all about the teaching component of the guided-reading model: what we do with that group of four, or five, or six, or more students sitting in front of us ready to be readers. It offers a collection of practical teaching routines for guided reading instruction at each of the four broad developmental stages: emergent readers (who are not yet connecting letters and sounds and who "read" mainly from pictures and memory); early readers (who are beginning to decode and recognize some words automatically); developing readers (for whom word-solving comes more automatically and flexibly, so they can devote more energy to higher-level comprehension and longer text); and fluent readers (who are building competence and confidence with increasingly sophisticated concepts, structures, and vocabulary). Each section includes a brief overview of the characteristics of readers at that stage, guidelines for selecting appropriate texts for those readers, a sampling of learning goals, and a collection of teaching ideas for helping students reach some of those goals. A chapter on guided reading for struggling readers in upper grades offers ideas on supporting reluctant readers to build the confidence and competence they need to be lifelong readers. The final chapters on nonfiction reading include ideas for teaching students to read informational text, as well as nontraditional and functional texts such as websites, directions, schedules, and even traffic signs.

In this book you will find a collection of practical teaching and learning routines to help make guided reading instruction more intentional, manageable, and engaging. There are many lessons, tips, ideas, and practice activities to meet a wide range of learning goals. You'll find ideas for sticky-note reading and the Reading Toolkit; active games for letter- and word-level study; graphic organizers and "foldables" for organizing and recording information; and techniques, such as "noisy punctuation" and "reading sliders," for building fluency. Although the routines have been organized by developmental stage, most can be modified to suit readers at different levels and for different purposes.

Guiding Readers: Making the Most of the 18-minute Guided Reading Lesson is the work of a reflective teacher, a lifelong learner—and a struggling student of Italian. I hope it will provide you with ideas for teaching, food for thought about your own practices, and encouragement to continue learning, growing, and taking risks in an ongoing effort to improve literacy instruction for all our students.

1

Guided Reading: What We Know Now

"Guided reading is not about levels, benchmark texts or offering the right prompts to students when they struggle with words. Rather guided reading is, for us, about supporting students as they develop strategic approaches to making meaning." (Burkins & Croft, 1990: xxi)

For many teachers in classrooms today, there has never been a time without guided reading as part of the literacy block. But there are still those of us who remember when a new approach to small-group instruction—some even called it "small-group reading recovery"—burst onto the scene. Irene Fountas and Gay Su Pinnell, pioneers of guided reading, defined this model as "a context in which a teacher supports each reader's development of effective strategies for processing texts at increasingly challenging levels of difficulty" (1996: 3). It was a radical departure for many of us who, at that time, had pretty much abandoned small-group instruction.

Borrowing from some of the principles of Reading Recovery, guided reading instruction incorporated needs-based groupings, texts of graduated levels of difficulty, and a focus on building independence in processing print. The guided reading lesson was a time for student reading, not teacher talk. As teachers, we were often reminded, "You have two ears but only one mouth," a wise admonition to listen twice as much as we talked. This time was an opportunity for readers to practice a range of strategies for negotiating texts that had been carefully chosen to provide just the right balance of challenge and support. The teacher's role was not to introduce new concepts or strategies, but to offer sensitive scaffolding and prompting as needed.

These strong principles of guided reading still apply today. But over the years, the term *guided reading* has come to mean different things to different people. As always, reflective practitioners are questioning their own practices. Are we providing an adequate balance of comprehension and word study? Do groups organized by reading level properly address a range of skill and strategy needs? Are guided reading lessons too structured—or not structured enough? How much and what kind of teacher talk is appropriate during guided reading?

As I focus more on *guiding readers* than *guided reading*, I am prepared to adapt instructional modes to meet the needs of my students.

In response to these concerns, teachers have developed alternative models of guided reading, calling them *strategy groups* or *differentiated reading groups*. The Florida Centre for Reading Research has made a distinction between guided reading and *skill-focused lessons*, which they describe as "teacher-planned lessons that provide the opportunity for more systematic and focused practice on a relatively small number of critical elements at a time" (Kosanovich, Ladinsky, Nelson, & Torgeson, 2006: 3), usually related to word study.

I believe that there is room for many variations within the guided-reading model. As I noted in the Introduction, my ideas of what guided reading looks like have not *changed* as much as *expanded* over the years. As I focus more on *guiding readers* than on an orthodoxy of guided reading, I am prepared to adapt instructional modes to meet the needs of my students. There is no one formula for what's right in guided reading. Small-group instruction will look different for different groups and in different situations.

Over the years, many of my perceptions about guided reading have changed. Like many teachers, I now look at independent-learning routines differently than I did in the past. My thinking about management and grouping has also evolved, as has my understanding of teaching, texts, talk, and time.

I used to…	*Now I…*
• view guided reading as an opportunity for students to read while I scaffolded them as necessary	• still emphasize supported processing of print during guided reading, but also incorporate purposeful skill and strategy work as necessary
• do limited planning for the guided reading lesson, choosing to teach from issues that arose solely from the reading	• do careful planning of the guided reading lesson, setting learning goals and planning instructional routines, but still remain open to the teachable moment
• treat each component of the literacy block—read-aloud, shared reading, guided reading, writing workshop, etc.—as separate	• strive to align the goals and routines of the literacy components so that each supports the other
• spend a lot of time and energy planning independent-learning activities for the students not involved in guided reading	• take time to establish independent routines of reading and writing, so students learn responsibility and self-regulation
• rely heavily on leveled reading materials as texts for guided reading instruction	• am experienced enough with supports and challenges in reading—and readers—to enable me to choose from a range of different texts
• look for texts that offered at least 90% support and 10% challenge to readers	• look for texts that offer at least 95% support, meet designated instructional goals, and are geared to the interests and background knowledge of the students
• allow limited time for student talk: usually just responses to teacher questions to assess comprehension	• allow extended time for authentic literate conversations, sometimes (but not always) prompted by "big-idea" questions.
• read a text once and move on to a new text	• revisit the text over at least two lessons to build comprehension and fluency
• teach reading during reading time and writing during writing time	• look for ways that reading and writing authentically support one another
• struggle with management of time and resources	• still struggle with management of time and resources, but continue to work on systems to support transitions, record-keeping, and teacher sanity

Harmonizing the Literacy Block

Too often in the past, there's been discord between small-group reading instruction and all the other components of the literacy block. Reading work in small groups often bore little connection to the learning that took place in read-aloud and shared reading, writing workshop, and independent centre work. And yet we know that literacy instruction is more effective if it's harmonized rather than piecemeal (Baumann & Ivey, 1995). In an integrated literacy block, guided reading is the practice piece—the "we do" in the guided release of responsibility (Pearson & Gallagher, 1993)—an opportunity for students to work with the strategies and concepts introduced during whole-class instruction, with appropriately challenging texts and targeted teacher support. For example, we might use the whole-class read-aloud to model a strategy like inferring. Then, during guided reading, each group can work on drawing inferences in their own reading. Not every group will be functioning at the same level of sophistication, but all will have an opportunity to practice the strategy as they process the print on their own.

Components of the Literacy Block
- Read-aloud
- Shared Reading
- Guided Reading
- Independent Reading
- Shared and Interactive Writing
- Writing Workshop

So, how does guided reading fit with the rest of the literacy block? Most jurisdictions mandate how much time should be dedicated to reading and writing instruction; some even recommend how that time should be parceled out into the various components of the program. Keep in mind that guided reading is only one piece of literacy instruction; not only do we not need to see every guided reading group every day but, in truth, we probably can't. Students still have opportunities to make sweet music with books through the other components of the literacy block.

A final word on scheduling: We want to schedule guided reading regularly and frequently. If we block our guided reading sessions in 20-minute chunks, that leaves us 18 minutes for the lesson and 2 minutes for transition. Perhaps a one-hour block three days a week works for you, or perhaps you can manage only 40-minute block three days a week. Maybe conducting guided reading every other day, or maybe four days a week, leaving the fifth for a catch-up day, is what works best for you. The key is consistency. And remember that the students are still learning even when they're not sitting with you in small-group instruction.

Independent Learning: Reading and Writing

The independent learning component of the guided-reading block should be self-directed and should involve students in independent practice of the learning goals of the guided reading lesson.

I cringe today to think about the amount of time and energy I used to devote to "what the other kids are doing." Often I spent more time planning those activities than it took the students to complete them! I really believed that I was providing authentic and rich learning experiences. But in reality, these experiences were often busy work that had little to do with the focus of the guided reading lesson or with making my students better readers, writers, thinkers, and independent learners. How often did my students work with me diligently on a particular strategy during the guided reading session, then move on to learning-centre work that was completely unrelated to what we had been practicing? Here's a radical thought: Maybe the independent learning component of the guided reading block should be self-directed, not teacher-dictated. And maybe it should somehow involve students independently engaging in what had been practiced with support in the guided reading lesson.

Three things to do during independent learning:

- Read
- Write
- A Must-do related to the guided reading lesson

Many teacher-writers have provided great advice about establishing independent learning routines:

Margot Southall, *Differentiated Learning Centres*

Joan Moser and Gail Bouchey, *The Daily Five*

Pat Pavelka, *Guided Reading Management*

Debbie Diller, *Literacy Work Stations*.

Easy-peasy texts present no challenges to the reader, either in accuracy or comprehension.

Just-right/Tiptoe texts will largely be accessible but will require the reader to stretch now and then.

Tough texts are too difficult for a reader to read on his/her own.

That's why today, my students have three alternatives for independent learning: reading, writing, and "must-do." The must-do (described more fully in chapter 2) is a teacher-designed learning activity intended to follow up on the guided reading lesson, another piece of the literacy block. It might involve further reading, working with a focus strategy, extended word work on a concept from the guided reading lesson, or extending the experience with the guided-reading text through written response. All the work on a comprehension strategy or word-solving skill is for naught if the students don't apply it when they are reading on their own. Each guided reading session is followed by a must-do that supports independent practice.

For the rest of their independent learning time, my students are reading or writing. Period. Gradually, we add variations, such as buddy reading, writing on the computer, theme box reading, or a choice menu of writing responses. Of course, it will come as no surprise to teachers reading this book that nothing is ever that simple in teaching or in life. It takes a lot of modeling, practicing, stamina-building, and reinforcement before students are able to engage independently in reading or writing for 20 minutes—but it is quite possible, even in Kindergarten. And it is well worth it.

A final word about independent learning: Take time to teach, to practice, to guide, and to backslide and teach again. It's likely to take several weeks or even months to establish the necessary routines, but trying to start small-group instruction before the rest of the students are ready to function independently will only create stress for everyone. And the time taken to build self-regulation will have payoffs well beyond the guided reading lesson.

Just-Right Reading

Probably the most difficult (and possibly the most important) part of planning a guided reading lesson is choosing the right text for the group.

Just-right texts for guided reading have students standing on their tiptoes. What a wonderful metaphor for the instructional reading level! Think about standing on your tiptoes. It's not that hard, but it does require some concentration and effort—and every now and then we might lose our balance and need some support. In the same way, instructional-level text is accessible with a little reading work and occasional scaffolding from the teacher. That's what instructional-level text does.

I used to call the instructional level "90-10 reading," based on a common standard of 90–95% accuracy. But now I think that even 10% challenge may be too great for many readers. To put things in perspective, think of it this way: *Charlotte's Web* has an average of about 200 words on each page. Reading at 90% accuracy means that there is an average of 20 difficult words *on every page!* Even at 96% accuracy, a reader would struggle with 8 words on every single page. (That gives a whole new meaning to "frustration level," doesn't it?)

So how do we find that tipping point between challenge and frustration? These days, I'm inclined to go back to Emmett Betts's original 1946 research, which recommends that instructional-level text be read at 95–98% accuracy, with adequate (75–89%) comprehension. We want our readers to be challenged, but not frustrated, so we should err on the side of too-easy rather than too-hard. Research tells us that readers gain much from reading accessible, easy-peasy texts, but texts that are too tough do nothing to help readers grow (Allington, 2006).

Independent Level	Instructional Level	Frustration Level
98–100% accuracy *and* thorough comprehension	95–98% accuracy *and* basic comprehension	Below 95% accuracy *or* inadequate comprehension

See page 119 for more information on the art and science of readability.

Now let's talk about leveling. We teachers need to be a lot more savvy, and perhaps less trusting, about published reading levels. I've always found leveled books to be a convenience for both instruction and assessment, and today we have available a richer selection of leveled books in a wider range of genres than ever before. However, I now know that I can't rely on a publisher to make the match between my readers and the best books for them.

Levels (or readability statistics, described in chapter 7) are simply guides to the supports and challenges offered by a particular text. But we've all had situations in which a group of students has coped easily with one text but struggled with another text at the same "level". That's because levels can tell us only what the book brings to the reading equation. A level number, letter, code, or name can't tell us what the readers bring—their background knowledge, their interest in the material, their ability to cope with the particular text structure. That's why it's important to know what leveling systems mean, as well as knowing what our students know and can do.

The other reason to be smart about text supports and challenges is that it opens the door to a range of instructional choices beyond leveled books. As long as we understand the strengths and needs of our students and can match them to the supports and challenges of a particular text, fiction and nonfiction trade books, chapter books, novels, environmental print, and even basal readers can also be used in the guided-reading program. For example, Chapter 9 of this book deals with using functional texts, such as directions, brochures, and websites, in the guided reading program.

For an in-depth explanation of book leveling, go to www.lorijamison.com, click on *Books* and scroll down to *Matching the Reader to the Text*.

Let me add a word of caution about using trade and functional literature for guided reading. Today's "leveling madness" has led to levels for everything from Dr. Seuss to Shakespeare. But trade books and novels were written to tell stories or relay information, not to teach children to read. They aren't likely to have such supports for developing readers as controlled vocabulary, purposeful line breaks, or regulated sentences. Furthermore, the level of difficulty from page to page or from chapter to chapter might fluctuate wildly. Assigning an average reading level or grade-level readability to an entire novel might well mean that some sections will be very easy and others will be far too difficult for students to read. That's not to say we can't use trade books or excerpts from novels, but we need to pay careful attention to the supports and challenges in each passage and be intentional about the routines we use to introduce and scaffold the learners.

There's one more consideration when choosing the just-right text for guided reading: does it meet the instructional goals of the lesson? In addition to an appropriate level of difficulty, I look for language, content, or text features that lend themselves to the lesson focus. For example, I might look for a text that contains many -*ed* and -*ing* words for a Grade 1 group working on inflectional endings, or a text that lends itself to confirming and adjusting predictions for a Grade 3 group practicing synthesis.

As teachers, we need to be a lot more savvy and perhaps less trusting about reading levels. We can't rely on publishers to make the match between our readers and the best books for them.

A final word on leveling: Books are leveled, not children. Levels are an instructional resource that guides us in knowing what challenges and supports a particular text offers readers. But all leveling tells us is what a book brings to the equation. Skillful teachers know how to make the magical instructional match that has children reading on their tiptoes, and how to re-balance them before they fall.

Time for Talk

Student talk is a very important part of the guided reading lesson. Many studies have linked talk about text to greater literacy growth (Langer, 1995; Dickinson & Smith, 1994). But not just any talk will do. If we want our students to become better readers, we need to engage them in more analytic talk—talk that involves drawing inferences, making judgments, asking (not just answering) questions, and digging deeper into the text.

Research tells us that most of the dialogue that traditionally has gone on in school was students responding to known-answer questions asked by the teacher (Cuban, 1993). But this type of talk rarely occurs in real life. Imagine asking friend what time a local restaurant opens for lunch when you already know the answer and, when your friend provides the correct response, saying, "Good job!"

Real dialogue occurs when participants listen and respond to what the others are saying. In their research on exemplary teachers, Richard Allington and his colleagues discovered that the best teachers encouraged a lot more purposeful student talk than that which occurred in less-successful classrooms (Allington, 2002). This talk was described as "conversational" rather than "interrogational." The teachers listened carefully to student talk and responded authentically, often probing the students for more information.

Literate conversations about books engage readers in talk about their own reading process.

Literate conversations about books may begin with summarizing the gist of the passage or noting key points, but they are also about critique, analysis, and personal response. Literate conversations engage readers in talk about their own reading processes—their questions, connections, inferences, predictions, mental images, and conclusions. The ability to be aware of and describe one's own thinking is called *metacognition*—thinking about one's own thinking—and is the essence of strategic reading. This is how readers build a repertoire of tools to draw on when they encounter roadblocks in their reading

One of the things I've learned is that I need to teach my students how to have a conversation. Many of them (even in high school) don't know how to listen and respond to someone else's ideas. I frequently pause to say, "Does anyone have a response to Jenny's idea before we talk about another idea?" I model summarizing another person's comments with "I think I heard you say…" or "Did you mean…?" I demonstrate how to courteously disagree with someone's *ideas* rather than with the person him- or herself. This teaching generally takes place outside the guided-reading setting, but is practiced and reinforced within the guided-reading group.

A final word on talk about text: Many people (this writer included) sort out their thoughts by talking through them. Other people prefer to gather their thoughts internally before expressing them publicly. Instead of punishing one student for monopolizing the conversation and another for not doing his or her part, we need to understand and extend each student's means of processing ideas. People have different needs for thinking through talk. Why not reframe the situation in a more positive, instructional way teaching loquacious Lori to stop and "talk to your brain" (see also page 53) before speaking aloud, and assuring quiet Quinn that it's safe to share his thoughts before they are fully formed?

Read It Again: Revisiting Texts

I took piano lessons as a youngster and still occasionally sit down to tickle the ivories (or plastics, as the case may be). Whether I'm playing "Happy Birthday" or "Moonlight Sonata," I know that I will have to play the piece over and over and over again before I can play it well.

When I first started working with guided reading, it never occurred to me to have the students read the same text more than once. My priority was to expose them to as many different texts as possible. And while I still want them to read a variety of books and other print materials, I know there is also great value in rereading the same text twice and even more times. There is extensive research on the power of rereading familiar text. Children as young as Kindergarten-age comprehend more deeply, comment more frequently, and respond more richly to texts that have been read more than once (Martinez & Roser, 1988).

Teacher-author Kelly Gallagher (2009: 98) suggests that the first reading of any text is simply "survival mode," in which readers are just accessing the print and getting control of the story. Deeper comprehension and higher-level response don't occur until the second or third "draft" of the reading

Multiple readings also benefit fluency. We need to play a piece of music on the piano several times to get it up to tempo and rhythm, and the same often goes for reading. The first sight-reading of the text enables the reader to solve unfamiliar words and negotiate meaning, freeing up the reader to focus on expression and phrasing in subsequent readings.

A final word on rereading familiar texts: We all know that some students balk at reading every word while reading a text a second time, much less any more. That's why it's important to provide a different purpose for each rereading. In the teaching routines in this book, I often indicate that a comprehension activity is to be done *after* the first reading: read to look for evidence to support character development, to find the main idea, etc. Reading manipulatives, such as pointers, framers, and highlighting tape (see Appendix page 162), often provide just the motivation that's needed to send a reader back into the text for another look.

The Reading–Writing Connection

In spite of the fact that we have long known that there is a connection between reading and writing, we have not always aligned them effectively in our instruction. When the National Reading Panel in the United States (NICHD, 2000) chose not to include the reading–writing connection in its meta-analysis of the research on reading instruction, writing was excluded from the national Reading First legislation and virtually disappeared from many primary classrooms. And yet it is clear that reading and writing develop simultaneously and each supports the development of the other.

There are many reasons to incorporate a writing component into small-group reading instruction (in addition to, not instead of, a separate writing block). A recent study of Kindergarten students found that interactive writing promoted phonological awareness, alphabet knowledge, and word reading (Jones, Reutzel & Fargo, 2010). When children write with invented spelling, stretching out words to write a letter for every sound they hear, they are developing both phonemic awareness and phonics in a natural and functional way.

Children as young as Kindergarten comprehend more deeply, comment more frequently, and respond more richly to texts that have been read more than once.

Reading and writing have a synergistic relationship: each supports the other to the extent that the whole is greater than the sum of the parts.

While reading is moving from letters to sounds, writing is moving from sounds to letters—and there is obvious overlap in these two processes. As David Pearson (2002) says in an interview with the National Writing Project, "Phonics is so much more transparent in spelling than it is in reading that I think it's easier for kids to deal with."

At more sophisticated levels, students can learn much about text structures and elements of the writer's craft from reading. Students often use themes, concepts, and structures from their reading in their own writing as they progress toward independence. On the other side of the coin, teaching students to generate written responses to reading helps them become metacognitive about their own reading processes and slows them down to think about their personal responses to the text.

Extended responses to reading as part of large-scale assessment is a reality of life for many students in upper grades. Unfortunately, too many students don't get the credit they deserve on these tests because they haven't learned how to craft an effective written response. This is an important part of the reading–writing connection. Adding a guided writing component to small-group reading instruction is sure to provide a payoff, both in terms of students' critical reading and their expressive writing.

A final word about the reading–writing relationship: It's more than just writing about reading. When we incorporate writing into the guided reading lesson, we teach about text structures and the writer's craft. We can talk about how segmenting a word to sound it out when reading is the same process as stretching out words to spell them when writing. The reading–writing connection must honor both reading and writing. As Lonna Smith (1998) wrote in her article on the reading–writing connection, "Integrated instruction results from participation in activities that promote the development of both."

The Reading-Writing Relationship

	Readers at this stage…	*Writers at this stage…*
Emergent	know that print tells a story and will role-play reading, making up their own stories or using a combination of pictures and memorizing	know that print tells a story and will role-play writing, using scribbles, pictures, and letter-like symbols to convey a message
Early	are starting to use letter–sound relationships to decode print	are starting to use letter–sound relationships to spell words
Developing	have mastered many mechanical elements of decoding so they enjoy and comprehend longer and more-complex texts	have mastered many mechanical elements of spelling and writing conventions and enjoy writing longer and more-complex texts
Fluent	are able to navigate longer, more-complex sentences and to interpret figurative language	are able to write longer, more-complex sentences and to use figurative language

2

The Guided Reading Lesson Sequence

Take a moment to picture a guided reading lesson in your mind. Do you see a group of children gathered on the reading rug, carefully tracking with their fingers as they whisper-read from the little books in front of them? Do you see a teacher and several children sitting around a table talking about their predictions about a story? Do you see group of children poring over books with magnifying glasses hunting for words? In truth, every one of these is a type of guided reading lesson—and there are many other variations, as well.

There is no single formula for an effective guided reading lesson. The content, process, and products of every lesson will vary according to the needs of the students in the group. That's what makes it such a wonderful tool for differentiating instruction.

As strong as an individual guided reading lesson can be, I believe we can get more bang for our pedagogical buck by thinking of guided reading as a sequence of three or four lessons based on the same text. We know that rereading familiar texts builds fluency and comprehension. We know that literate talk supports metacognition and higher-level thinking. We know that meaningful integration of reading and writing increases the proficiency of both. It's pretty difficult to achieve all of these things in one 18-minute lesson, but a series of lessons enables us to spend meaningful time with a text and achieve a number of literacy goals.

A *guided reading sequence* is a set of lessons on specific learning goals or areas of focus; it is based on the needs of the students, using a carefully chosen instructional-level text and learning experiences that stem from and build on connected reading. The guided reading sequence generally includes these stages:

> A guided reading sequence generally consists of three or more lessons with the same text.

Day 1: Text introduction and first reading—focus on basic accuracy and understanding

Day 2: Rereading of text—focus on comprehension and word study

Day 3 (and sometimes more): Rereading of text—extension of thinking, focus on text structures or writer's craft, often includes a writing experience

Although there is a general pattern to the lesson *sequence,* individual guided reading lessons will vary according to the needs of the learners, the goals of the lesson, and the nature of the text.

See page 30 for a template for planning a lesson sequence; page 29 for a sample plan.

Planning a Guided Reading Lesson Sequence

Given a brief window of only 18 minutes with a group of students, we want to make the most of our time by balancing careful planning and spontaneous teachable moments. It's important to start with a plan, but also to be flexible enough to provide just-in-time teaching to address immediate issues that arise from the reading. Preplanning a sequence of three or more lessons enables us to maximize both teaching time and planning time. Starting with the learning goals and appropriate texts, we can then consider how to use the myriad actions in the reading process to help our students become more proficient readers, writers, and thinkers.

Start with Learning Goals

What do we want our students to know and be able to do as a result of this lesson? The guided reading lesson is about supporting readers as they develop a range of processes for making meaning from texts. Sometimes the lesson will focus on a particular strategy or word-solving skill; at other times we will work on integrating several strategies to make sense of the reading. As Linda Hamilton Mudre suggests, "we want our students to command a well-balanced repertoire of reading operations and be able to choose specific actions that are well-suited to the problem at hand" (2003: 130). But for students to add these specific actions to their reading repertoire, they need modeling, reinforcement, and guided support. Small-group guided reading instruction is an opportunity to practice those actions with accessible texts and teacher scaffolding.

In planning a guided reading sequence, I prefer to include both text-level and word-level comprehension goals. In some circles, *comprehension* has been inexplicably separated from *word study*. But what part of word study doesn't involve comprehension? The reading process is a complex network of many systems, including deciphering those little marks on the page, that ultimately lead to making meaning from text. We want our students to have all of these systems in their reading repertoires, along with the knowledge of how and when to use them. The guided-reading framework enables us to embed word study into the context of connected reading. We want our students to understand that the reason we study a letter pattern or inflectional ending is not to be able complete a worksheet or answer a teacher's question, but to be able to understand what they read.

Beginning with learning goals enables us to target instruction and text selection to the specific strengths and needs of the readers in the group. Knowing that a group of students can competently read a Level 9 text gives us some information about them as readers, but it doesn't tell us what those students need to learn in order to be able to read a Level 10 text. Incorporating specific learning goals into the guided reading lesson sequence ensures that students are not missing important steps on the literacy journey.

Find the Right Text

As discussed in the previous chapter, one of the foundations of guided reading is the essential text–reader balance that has readers "standing on their tiptoes" to process the print. This balance of 95% support and 5% challenge is called instructional-level text because it is considered to be optimal for extending readers just enough to increase their competence. Plenty of easy-peasy text (see page 12) is essential for reading practice (in the same way that water that allows us to touch bottom when we need to is necessary to learning to swim). Tackling text that is too difficult contributes nothing to reading proficiency (and may cause

For the Guided Reading Lesson Plan template, see page 30.

For a sample guided reading lesson plan, see page 29.

damage by shattering fragile confidence). Tough text is intended for read-aloud and shared reading, not guided or independent reading.

Text difficulty or level is one important consideration, but it is not the only factor in choosing a particular passage for a particular lesson. We need to find texts that will support our instructional goals: for example, if we want students to practice confirming and adjusting predictions, we must ensure that the text lends itself to ongoing predictions; if we want students to decode words by syllables, we should find a text with plenty of multisyllabic words; if we want students to learn about procedural text structures, we need to choose reading material that contains directions or instructions.

Leveled books can be a valuable resource because we know that they will contain certain supports for children learning to read. But fiction and nonfiction trade books, magazine articles, and excerpts from novels can also be suitable guided reading texts—as long as the reading level is appropriate. We should also consider nontraditional texts from the world of functional reading, such as websites, schedules, brochures, recipes, or street signs.

Guided reading texts should be short. Entire novels or chapter books are usually inappropriate for guided reading for a number of reasons. For one thing, it is rare to have an entire novel at a consistent reading level. Even if we find one chapter at the students' instructional level, there's a good chance that the next chapter will be too difficult. Moreover, if we're going to use the guided reading sequence to read and reread the same chunk of text several times, it will take a very long time—and a lot of tedium—to complete an entire novel. Close reading and rereading of an entire novel would cause students to lose interest long before the story is done. However, there's nothing wrong with using a single chapter or excerpt from a novel for guided reading. In fact, sometimes reading one or two chapters of a novel in a guided reading session can provide enough support for students to read the rest of the book on their own.

Prepare a Text Introduction

The book introduction is the bridge between the readers and the text. A good book introduction establishes a context for the reading and activates prior knowledge. It's like opening an existing folder in the reader's mental computer to add another file. I think the book introduction is so important that, even after teaching for many years, I still prepare and make notes on what I'm going to say.

As independent readers, we almost always preview a text in some way before reading it. We might read the back cover or flyleaf blurb, check out the author's credentials, look at some reviews, or simply skim a small section to get a flavor of the prose. These previewing actions might spur us to read on—or to reject the book as uninteresting or unreadable. Students in guided-reading groups don't have access to most of these previewing supports, and certainly don't have the option of deciding that the designated passage doesn't meet their needs or interests. So it's up to the teacher to provide the necessary pegs to hook the students into the text.

I like to think of the book introduction as having three Ps: Preview, Purpose for reading, and Prior knowledge. A text *preview* can be as simple as a one-sentence summary or as detailed as a page-by-page picture walk through the book, discussing what we see in each of the illustrations and introducing key vocabulary. The nature of the book introduction depends a lot on the *purpose* for reading. In

Entire novels or chapter books are not suitable for guided reading, but excerpts or chapters can be used effectively.

Teaching students to preview texts independently (see Do-It-Yourself Picture Walk on page 51, Get HIP to Reading on page 134, and What We Think We Know on page 134) helps them access any text they choose to read.

Three Ps Book Introduction
- Preview
- Purpose
- Prior knowledge

a guided reading lesson, we want to tell students upfront why they are reading this text; for example, to find out what happens to the character, to track our wonderings as we read, to talk to our brains about what we're reading, to gather facts about a particular topic. We want students to set their own goals for reading and be able to adjust their reading rate and style to the purpose for reading.

Activating *prior knowledge* is the other key step in the introduction. It has been well established that prior knowledge, background information, or schema is important to comprehension; in fact, it might have more impact on comprehension than reading ability itself (Langer, 1984). Prior knowledge includes all the information a reader has accumulated on a topic. Activating prior knowledge can be as simple as discussing "what we already know about this topic," drawing analogies to another book, or inviting students to make a connection to a personal experience.

Often, novice or struggling readers either don't have the background information required to understand a particular text or they don't know how to access the information they need. In this case, another prereading P—*preteaching*—is needed. Discussion or explicit teaching might be required to provide necessary information or vocabulary. Vocabulary is best taught in the context of the reading, rather than before reading (Fisher & Blachowicz, 2005). But when certain words are critical to understanding the overall text and there is not enough contextual support for students to solve them on their own, it might be necessary to preteach those words. If missing a particular word is unlikely to interfere with the meaning and appreciation of the text, let students use their strategies to solve the word independently—and then revisit the word after reading to review and reinforce.

Map Out Lesson Routines

Lesson routines are the actions we take to achieve the learning goals. Unlike a one-shot activity, a routine represents a behavior or habit of mind, such as sorting and categorizing, blending sounds, predicting and confirming, tracking thinking, or navigating nonlinear text.

The dozens of lesson routines in this book are organized by stage of literacy development and all are linked to specific learning goals; however, almost every one of them can be adapted to a variety of goals at a range of levels. As part of the lesson routine, we predetermine pause points in the text and guiding questions to probe and extend students' thinking. But the guided reading lesson represents a delicate balance of careful planning and spontaneous learning. Plans need to be flexible enough to seize the teachable moments that arise from the students' reading and to allow us to provide the just-in-time teaching that the guided reading framework affords.

Plan Must-Do Tasks for Follow-Up

Must-do activities can

- engage students in further reading to continue to apply the focus strategies independently
- provide opportunities to apply focus strategies independently
- extend students' experience with the text through written responses or further reading
- involve students in word or letter work based on the lesson focus

Every guided reading lesson is followed by a must-do routine or activity that provides students with an opportunity to independently (or with a partner) practice the learning they practiced with teacher support in the lesson. Students *must do* the must-do before moving on to other independent learning routines.

The must-do might involve word hunts or sound sorts, sticky-note strategy reading with a new text, written responses, or a range of other practices to reinforce learning. Each of the teaching routines in this book includes at least one idea for a must-do to follow the lesson. Not only does the must-do give students an opportunity for independent practice, it also provides a way for us to assess their mastery of a particular strategy or skill.

The Teacher in Guided Reading: Prompting and Questioning

It is generally agreed that the guided reading session is not the time for introducing new concepts and strategies. What, then, is appropriate teacher talk in a guided reading lesson?

During guided reading, teachers are most actively involved in prompting, questioning, and explaining. When we teach, we model and describe reading behaviors; when we prompt, we assume that students already know these behaviors—and the language to talk about them—so we give them a nudge to apply what they know. If students don't understand or apply a particular reading behavior that has been previously taught, additional explanation or teaching will be necessary. And that's one thing the guided reading lesson is for: providing small-group instruction that is not needed or not appropriate for the rest of the class. We need not feel guilty about some teacher talk in the guided reading lesson, as long as we keep in mind that the operative word in guided reading is *reading*.

That's why much of the teacher's time and energy during the guided reading lesson is devoted to prompting as students engage in reading and discussion. Prompting can occur in a variety of settings. We might prompt students to "tell more" when they are retelling a story; we might prompt students to provide evidence from the text for an opinion or idea; we frequently prompt students to correct themselves when they make a miscue.

The art of teaching is to provide prompting in such a way that it builds independence. For starters, we must allow time for a reader to correct a miscue on his/her own. If we intervene as soon as the child makes an error, we are teaching him/her to depend on us for deciding whether the words are right or not. As a rule, we tend to let capable readers miscue without intervening, because we are confident they will ultimately make sense of the text. But with struggling readers, we often jump in practically before they get the word out of their mouths. They learn to read hesitantly, never knowing when we are going to interrupt them. In effect, we are teaching them to be dysfluent!

When a student miscues and does not self-correct, guide him/her to use existing word-solving strategies with prompts:

- *Does that make sense to you? What word might make sense here? How do you know?*
- *See if the sounds in the word match the letters on the page.*
- *What clues are on the page to help you?*
- *Does that word look like a word you already know?*

It's difficult to anticipate what forms of prompting we will have to do during the guided reading lesson. These are teacher actions that arise spontaneously. But we can plan some of the questions we will ask to extend students' thinking before, during, and after the reading. Although we are all cognizant of the importance of asking higher-cognitive (interpretive, evaluative, inferential) questions, the truth is that we ask lower-cognitive (literal) questions most of the time. The guided-reading plan should include powerful "big idea" questions that probe students' thinking and stretch their reasoning, even for our youngest readers. If we

Teaching involves modeling and describing reading behaviors. Prompting happens after the teaching has taken place.

When a student makes a miscue, count for 3 to 5 seconds or allow the student to finish the page before prompting, to give him/her time to self-correct.

Research says that teachers wait an average of one second between asking a question and providing the answer or moving on. For low-level questions, the optimal wait time is three seconds. For high-level questions, there seems to be no optimal wait time. The longer we wait, the more likely students are to provide deeper answers. (Northwest Education, 1988) want our students to become more metacognitive, critical, and thoughtful readers, we need to focus on extending their thinking about both the text and the reading process. One way to do that is by waiting—both after asking the question and after hearing the response. In fact, research suggests that the longer we wait, the more likely students are to provide more elaborated and insightful responses. (Cotton, 1988).

Sometimes simply waiting after the reader has responded will motivate him/her to elaborate on the initial response. As an alternative, we can prompt or probe their thinking, inviting them to expand or explain, to offer support from the text, or to clarify their reasoning by asking questions:

- *How do you know?*
- *Why do you think so?*
- *What is the evidence in the text?*
- *And what else do you think?*

A good rule of thumb is to never stop at just one question. Always follow up a response with another question, prompt, or invitation to elaborate, even if that prompt is, "I know you don't know, but if you did know, what would you say?"

The Student in Guided Reading: Reading and Talking

To say that a student's actions in the guided reading lesson are "reading and talking" might be oversimplifying things a bit, but it's a good reminder that the bulk of that 18-minute lesson should be devoted to readers processing connected text. Even our beginning readers need to see that the purpose of the reading lesson is…well, reading. That's why we get them interacting with books—talking about pictures, chiming in for familiar phrases, recognizing symbols in print—even before they are able to connect letters and sounds to form words.

In the guided reading lesson, every reader should have his or her own copy of the text. After the text introduction, each reader reads independently, with the teacher listening in on the students briefly one by one. Some teachers, concerned with hearing every child read, have fallen into the round-robin reading trap. This traditional approach—having each student read aloud in turn from a text that they have never read before—has been universally panned by reading experts as contributing nothing to reading growth (but contributing much to damaged self-confidence and motivation). First-draft reading in front of an audience does not allow the reader the privacy or the time to apply strategies to solve difficult words or fix up comprehension mix-ups, or to reflect on the meaning of the text. Moreover, the students are unlikely to be doing much reading work themselves when it's not their turn to read. No one ever learned to become a better reader this way.

Instead, have students read privately, at their own pace. Emergent and early readers do not read silently; they need the auditory feedback of their own voices to know what they're reading. Teachers have many creative approaches to avoiding a chorus of readers: *reading phones* (elbows of PVC pipe) keep student's voices low by causing an echo in their own ears; *stagger starts* have students reading in different places in the text at any given time.

It's important to teach young readers that when they get to the end of the book they get to go back and start all over again! I tell the students to see how many times they can read the whole text before I tell them they have to stop. In this way, beginning readers are getting crucial bulk reading practice.

Students should never be asked to publicly read a text that they are reading for the first time.

While the students are reading, I simply tap a student's book to indicate he/she should raise his/her voice a little for me to hear. (Debbie Diller, author of *Literacy Work Stations,* suggests moving behind the students and looking over their shoulders as they read, encouraging them to focus on their texts rather than on you.) Sometimes I will ask a reader to go back and read a previous page so I can assess how well he or she has handled a particular challenge. I need to listen for only a few seconds, then move on to the next student. In this way, I can listen to each student two or three times during the course of the 18-minute lesson.

Developing- and fluent-stage readers might be asked to do their individual first-readings silently, or orally in a soft voice. When students are reading silently, they usually read only short chunks of text at a time (perhaps a page or two, depending on the amount of print on the page) then pause to discuss or strategize. However, I listen to them in the same way I listen to younger readers, by tapping a student's book with my hand to signal that he/she should read in a soft voice, just loud enough for me to hear.

TTYN: Talk to your Neighbor

Partner sticks are an easy, efficient, fair way to randomly pair students for partner work, using ordinary craft sticks. Use colored markers to paint the bottom of each stick so that there are two sticks in each color. Each student draws a partner stick at random and automatically becomes partnered with the person who has drawn the same-colored stick.

In the preceding chapter, we discussed the importance of talk in supporting reading development. In this book, you'll see frequent references to TTYN or "Talk to Your Neighbor." Much of the talk we do in guided-reading groups is done with partners. Often we will use the Think, Pair, Share strategy, in which individuals are given a few moments to reflect on a problem or question, then invited to discuss their ideas with a partner before sharing the discussion with the whole group.

Even in a group of four to six, it's possible for some individuals to dominate the discussion and others to tune out. When students talk to a partner, they are more likely to get 50% of the talk time—and are more accountable for sharing, participating, and taking turns. When students have the opportunity to talk to a partner, they sort out their thinking, negotiate their ideas, and rehearse their talk. As teachers, we can easily monitor (and sometimes intervene or participate in) three separate conversations to assess students' comprehension, metacognition, and communication. Then we can decide whether we want to bring the discussion back to the whole group, or leave it at partner talk. Among the advantages of partner talk before group discussion is that students have a chance to clarify their thinking so the group talk is more articulate and focused.

The Guided Reading Lesson Sequence

The guided reading sequence is founded on the best that we know about teaching: offering a balance of text-level and word-level comprehension practice in the context of accessible texts; using assessment to guide learning experiences that stretch every student just beyond where he/she is; revisiting familiar texts to increase comprehension and fluency; offering just-in-time teaching to address the needs that arise on the spot. It may very well be the most powerful teaching that we do.

We generally spend at least two to three days with the same text—and sometimes more, depending on the richness of the text and the goals for reading it. We read the text first for meaning and then for deeper analysis. It is by revisiting the text that we teach students to build layers of comprehension.

Day 1: Text Introduction and First-Draft Reading

The first day of a guided reading sequence is generally occupied by the book introduction and the students' independent first reading of the text. When texts are very short and/or the text preview very brief, students can usually read through the text more than once.

Remember that the first reading of a text is the opportunity for readers to process the print and get the gist of the message, so try to minimize interruptions during the first reading. Deeper understanding usually emerges from further encounters with the text (assuming that the content of the text lends itself to any depth). The exception to this rule occurs when you want students to predict, to wonder, or to apply other processes that must take place during the first reading. You might have students track their thinking with sticky notes, but you don't want to interfere with their overall understanding of the passage.

Day 1 of the lesson sequence often ends with a retelling and/or a brief discussion of the passage. By this point, it's likely that the 18-minute timer has sounded, and you need to explain the group's must-do before we all move on to the next group.

Day 2: Dipping Back into the Text

The second day of the guided reading sequence generally focuses on deeper comprehension and processing of the text. Start by rereading the text—independently, in buddies, or occasionally in chorus. Spend a few minutes revisiting the previous day's must-do and providing students with an opportunity to share their work with others. The second day of reading might address specific comprehension strategies, revisiting sections of the text to talk about inferences, mental images, questions, or connections. For upper-level readers, this day is an opportunity to dip back into specific sections of the book as you talk about both the text and the reading process. With beginning readers, you are more likely to dip into the text to focus on specific word and letter features, hunting for words that contain specific letters or patterns.

But whether you're engaging in literate talk, working with words in isolation, or crafting written responses, you always need to bring it back to the book. Individual elements of the guided reading sequence are useful only when students understand how each one supports integrated, meaningful, connected reading for the task at hand and beyond. Always, the ultimate goal of any guided reading lesson is to help students develop strategic independence.

Some discussion will arise naturally out of the reading, but it's also important to plan big-idea questions that extend students' thinking and enrich their experience with the text. Teachers can support analytic talk by asking thoughtful questions, probing for more information, and requiring readers to offer evidence from the text. In her book *Reading Power,* Adrienne Gear (2006) calls this the BIBB strategy—always "bring it back to the book."

As always, the lesson ends with a must-do—further practice on the word- or text-level strategy, extended experiences with the text, or revisiting the text for fluency practice.

For building deeper comprehension and communication, never stop at just one question. Take every student response one step further by asking another question, prompting the speaker to elaborate or inviting support for the response.

Day 3: Thinking Beyond the Words

As always, begin by reviewing the must-do from the previous day and rereading portions of the text that will have particular application for that day's lesson. Examples of revisiting for the purpose of reading beyond the text:

- word-hunting to focus on a particular print feature or letter pattern
- examining unique text structures, such as a table of contents, speech bubbles, or charts
- focusing on illustrations and their role in telling a story or conveying information
- revisiting a prereading activity to confirm predictions or prior knowledge
- studying figurative language or literary techniques

Depending on the richness of the text and the purposes for reading, a guided reading sequence might even extend beyond three days. Usually the last day in the sequence will involve an experience with shared, interactive, or guided writing. This can be as simple as generating word lists or building sentences, or as elaborate as crafting a reading response or text innovation. Just as readers can clarify their thinking by writing, writers can learn about craft by reading. This is a powerful opportunity to enrich students' lives as readers, writers, and thinkers.

Tips, Tools, and Techniques

There used to be times when I felt like one of those circus clowns who balance several spinning plates on sticks while riding a unicycle. Some things don't change. Keeping all those curricular plates up in the air will always be a challenge.

As I visit classrooms across North America, I sometimes think that elementary teachers have an organization gene not present in most of the general population. But perhaps I'm not the only one who has had to interrupt a guided reading lesson to grab a dry-erase marker or to search for a missing book or to reprimand a student who is off-task. Managing time, managing materials, and managing assessment and record-keeping are all challenges that can become unwieldy without consistent systems in place.

Here, we'll look at a few simple practices that help me keep on track and make the most of not only those precious 18 minutes with a guided-reading group, but my precious preparation time as well.

1. Establish Routines

It all boils down to routines and procedures: routines for independent learning, routines for handling materials, routines for seeking help for problems.

Almost 30 years ago, Pearson and Gallagher (1983) identified an instructional model they called the *gradual release of responsibility*, which suggested that new learning is most effectively mastered when it shifts incrementally from the teacher as model, to student practice with teacher support, to independent application by the student. This principle applies as much to behaviors as it does to cognition. Start by showing and explaining to students what is expected of them. Give them plenty of opportunity to practice with support before expecting them to engage in the routine independently.

Reading and writing have a symbiotic relationship; each strengthens the other.

Gail Bouchey and Joan Moser (2005) describe a system for "building muscle memory" that includes a stage they call *stamina-building*, in which children are expected to participate in each routine for longer and longer time periods until they achieve mastery for an extended period of time. Some teachers display charts on which they graph the number of minutes all students can work independently without interruption, waiting until the entire class can reach the magic 18-minute mark before small-group instruction even begins.

Even the most independent learners will need time to master the classroom routines necessary for a guided-reading program to run smoothly. We need to give our students—and ourselves—time to establish those independent learning routines. It usually takes six to eight weeks, during which time we can be conducting assessments and teaching through read-alouds, shared reading, independent reading, and writing workshop. You will find it is well worth the time to establish that student self-regulation, with or without guided reading.

2. Minimize Transition Times

Transitions can be a major time-waster, one that is easily eliminated by establishing routines for moving from one activity to another. That's where the 18-minute timer comes in. One of the earliest routines I establish is for all of us to listen for the "two-minute warning" to signal the end of a 20-minute guided reading session. For me, it's a signal to wrap up the lesson, explain the must-do, and get ready for the next group. For the students, it's a signal to put away their materials and move on to the next activity.

The key, of course, is to make sure that students know what to do with their materials and where to go next. Those are the routines that we model, demonstrate, and practice, practice, practice. I'm noticing that an increasing number of teachers, especially those with younger students, like to bring the whole class together at the end of each guided reading lesson. They might do a shared reading of a poem, read a story, or simply "shake the sillies out" before moving to the next guided reading lesson. These students know to gather at the class meeting spot and wait for the teacher's direction.

I teach students to bring their individual book boxes to the guided-reading table and read independently until I am ready to start the guided reading lesson. Individual book boxes generally contain the current guided-reading text; copies of three or four previous texts; some independent-reading materials, such as library books; perhaps a folder of weekly poems; and sometimes a reading journal or other collection of personal writing. When I introduce a new guided-reading text, I ask students to return one of old texts from their book boxes. This simple routine engages students in connected reading and frees me up for a few minutes to deal with issues in the class or to conduct an oral reading record with one of the students in the group.

3. Eliminate Interruptions

I know, I know, it seems pretty obvious! But I've had teachers ask me well into the school year how to eliminate interruptions during guided reading. Unfortunately, by that time, students have had months to train their teacher to be interrupted! It should be the other way around. You need to train students to seek assistance from other students or to move on to other work if they encounter a problem they can't fix. One of the many advantages of simple independent

Plastic magazine holders make durable (but costly) individual book boxes, while cardboard magazine holders and even empty laundry detergent boxes are much more economical alternatives.

I've seen teachers use many creative techniques for reminding students not to interrupt the guided reading lesson, from wearing a firefighter's hat labeled SOS (for emergencies), to wearing a tiara ("When the queen is busy, she's not to be bothered"), to holding up a large plastic Stop sign.

learning routines, such as "read or write," is that every task should be within the students' capabilities. And having students practice and rehearse routines until they're mastered before we expect independence assures that there will be less need to seek help from the teacher.

One of my preferred routines is to provide a collection of bright yellow sticky notes labeled "*HELP!*" If a student needs teacher assistance, he/she places the sticky note on his/her desk or table and moves on to something else: this is another routine that involves plenty of modeling and practice. When I'm free, I scan the room for the yellow stickies and can take a few moments to address the issues. (Amazingly, the majority of these crises are solved or long-forgotten by that point.)

4. Build In Assessment

Basically, there are two main types of assessment data for guided reading: anecdotal notes and oral reading records (running records with comprehension checks). It's also possible to evaluate some of the must-do tasks. You can use the first few minutes of each lesson to take a quick oral reading record with one student while others read from their book boxes. Usually this oral reading record is conducted with the current guided-reading text, but there's no reason you can't use an unfamiliar leveled text, such as a benchmark book, for a more formal assessment.

It's hard to find time during the guided reading lesson for making anecdotal records. While it can be handy to jot notes right on the lesson plan, teachers have a range of other tools for anecdotal records, from notebooks with a tab for each student to sticky notes that are later transferred to file folders. I have a file folder containing a library pocket for each student, so the whole class is right there in one folder. The library pockets are just the right size for holding 3" x 5" index cards, which I can pull out to jot dated observations about students, to record running record data, etc. When one card is full, I just add another card to the pocket.

I like to change my groups once a month. As I approach the end of the month, I might even cancel guided reading for a day or two and allow students to work independently so that I can catch up on individual reading records. We need to remind ourselves that assessment is legitimate use of instructional time! As I approach the end of the month, I'll also take a quick look at my anecdotal notes; if there are students whose cards contain a dearth of information, I make a point of observing those students more closely for a few days.

At the end of the month, I analyze all the student information cards and physically reshuffle them to form new guided-reading groups for the next month.

5. Manage Materials

I don't think I could live without my timer and my four-drawer plastic storage cart! I confess that I'm married to my timer (a spouse that never argues with me) and couldn't do without it. Keeping my guided reading lessons at 18 minutes helps balance my whole day.

Because I prefer to work with four guided-reading groups, I use one drawer in my cart for each group. In the drawer is everything I need for the entire guided reading sequence over two to three lessons: my lesson plan; a copy of the text for each student; reading manipulatives we will use, such as plastic letters, dice,

Sometimes, if I need to have five groups, I'll place an extra basket on the top of my storage cart. But I won't have more than five groups. Having too many groups makes meeting times too infrequent and too widely spaced for continuity.

whiteboards and markers. I want to have all the materials at my fingertips to keep the lesson flowing smoothly and the time flowing efficiently.

Sticky-Note Reading and the Reading Toolkit

Among the materials we need are different sizes and shapes of sticky notes. As students read, they can track their thinking with sticky notes, tabbing specific points of interest or strategy spots in a text during reading. Sticky-note reading helps readers engage with text and think about what they are doing as they read. It requires them to consciously apply strategies to solve reading mix-ups, to be metacognitive; in other words, to think about their thinking. And most importantly, it builds readers who are active participants, not passive recipients, in reading.

Sticky-note reading can be used to support whatever comprehension strategy you are working on in the guided reading lesson: questioning, connecting, inferring, predicting, visualizing, etc. Highlighting tape can also be used to draw attention to specific words or letter features in the text.

One of the challenges of sticky-note reading is managing all those little scraps of paper. In an 18-minute guided reading lesson, we simply don't have time to waste searching for or distributing sticky notes. If we are going to make the most of our time, we need to have all our supplies at our fingertips.

My easy and inexpensive solution is the Reading Toolkit (see pictures in margin), stocked with sticky notes, that enables me to access these tools quickly and efficiently. Sometimes I will provide a variety of stickies from which students may choose, and other times I will have the toolkits prestocked with the specific size or type of sticky notes that will be needed for that day's reading.

Reading Toolkits are simple to create from a colored file folder. With the file folder shut, cut it in 10 cm (3") strips. This gives you four Toolkits from one file folder. Add a clipart label, if you choose, and laminate the Toolkit for durability. Add a plastic coil for a pencil at the top (small golf pencils are just the right size) and you're set to stock the Toolkit with sticky notes for active reading.

Prestocking the Reading Toolkit with sticky notes eliminates time wasted in handing out materials. I store the Toolkits in my four-drawer organizer and distribute them along with the books at the beginning of the guided reading lesson. Additional Reading Toolkits can be available to students for independent reading as well.

Tools for sticky-note reading
- various sizes, colors, and shapes of sticky notes
- sticky-note Stop sign
- strips of highlighting tape
- colored flags
- pencil or pen

Guided Reading Lesson Plan

Group: Haley, Jaleesa, Raj,
Stella, Janie, Chelsea

Date: 15/10/10

Title/Level	Learning Goals
All Clean. mid-early	Comprehension: retelling - characterizations - self monitoring Text structure: speech bubbles Fluency - ~~and~~ phrases

Text Introduction

Preview: book about Marion who loves to clean
cover - parrot, vacuum cleaner, window
pic flic - speech bubbles, vocab - vacuum, parrot

Prior Knowledge: TTYN - when did you help clean
the house?
build words - clean (cleaning) cleaner) - mix + fix

Purpose: Read to see what the problem is and how
it is solved.

Day 1	Must-Do
Text preview - Word building - c, l, e, a, n First reading, stagger start Use sliders for phrasing Remind - 3 cueing syst. first retell.	- cut up story - reassemble pictures + add text.

Day 2	Must-Do

- review must-do.
 - reread text
 - Retelling map ADD
 - share your favourite
    page
 - What do you know about
    Marion?
	- story souvenir: feather
	
	 - retelling cubes in
	    partners

Day 3 (Int. Writing speech bubbles)	Must-Do
- reread text - Word decisions er, ed, ing - blends cl - play shower curtain game? HF words	- add sticky note speech bubbles and write what the characters would say

Guided Reading Lesson Plan

Group: Date:

Title	Learning Goals

Text/Book Introduction

Preview:

Prior Knowledge:

Purpose:

Day 1	Must-Do
Day 2	**Must-Do**
Day 3	**Must-Do**

Pembroke Publishers ©2012 *Guiding Readers* by Lori Jamison Rog ISBN 978-1-55138-273-9

3

Guiding Emergent Readers

During free choice time in Kindergarten, Mai always goes straight to the reading corner. She knows where to find her favorite books—usually those that have been read to her in class and at home. Already, Mai has definite reading preferences; at the moment, she is crazy about Fancy Nancy books. In fact, judging by her matching socks, skirt, and hair ribbon, she's something of a Fancy Nancy herself! As she flips the pages of a book, Mai can be heard animatedly telling the story to herself, sometimes with the words she has heard read to her and sometimes with her own inventions.

Like most Kindergarten students, Mai is described as an *emergent reader*. Sometimes called *role-play readers,* children at this stage don't yet know sound–symbol correspondences, so they can't negotiate print in a conventional way. But they do know a lot of things about reading and writing, and will often pretend to read. In fact, we can often hear our own voices and inflections coming back to us in their reading!

Many emergent readers will be able to print their own names and recognize some alphabet letters. They might even be able to identify some words. It's interesting that, at this stage, certain words are pictographs in the reader's mind, so the word they recognize in one context will not be recognized in other contexts (for example, the word *Crest* on the toothpaste tube).

Emergent Readers

- know that print tells a story or gives information
- may have mastered certain concepts about print, such as distinguishing the front of the book from the back or the text from the pictures.
- may be able to sing the alphabet song or identify individual letters, but are not connecting letters and sounds to negotiate print
- may be able to recognize and write their own names
- often role-play reading, turning the pages and using a distinct storytelling voice
- "read" from memory and pictures
- can usually tell about something that has been read to them
- write to communicate or tell a story, using scribbles, letters, or letter-like symbols

Texts for Emergent Readers

Emergent readers are not yet negotiating print, so they rely on texts that are repetitious and have solid support for illustrations. Generally speaking, the text simply labels the pictures, from one word (*dog, bird, mouse*) to complete sentences (*Here is a red dog. Here is an orange bird.*) In more challenging text, the pattern might change on the last page (*The animals are playing.*)

Other characteristics of emergent level texts:

- mostly nonfiction (labeling of pictures) rather than having a storyline
- topics and themes within the experience of young children
- heavily predictable, with a repeated pattern
- strong illustrative support for key vocabulary
- from one to two short lines of print per page
- enlarged print and spacing
- print found in the same place on every page

Sun Fun by Elle Ruth Orav, illustrated by Lam Quach (2001). Reprinted courtesy of Curriculum Plus Publishing.

The Guided Reading Lesson for Emergent Readers

See page 45 for a sample guided reading lesson plan for emergent readers.

The guided reading lesson looks a little different for emergent readers than for any other stage of development. After all, these students don't actually know how to process print. In fact, some teachers would argue that these students aren't ready for guided reading. But there are many things we can do to support emerging literacy skills in the small-group guided reading lesson. We might work on letter naming, retelling, or spaces around words, all in the context of connected text. We don't need to wait until students have mastered concepts about print or letter–sound relationships before putting a book in their hands and letting them access the story within.

The first step, of course, is to establish independent learning routines. With time and patience, even our youngest students can be taught to engage with books independently for 20 minutes while the teacher is working with a guided-reading group. They learn that when they hear the 18-minute timer, they should put away what they are working on, gather their individual book boxes (see chapter 2), and come to the designated meeting spot. For the students in the guided reading group, the routine is to read from individual book boxes until the teacher is ready to start the lesson. This gives the teacher time to sort out issues with the independent learning group, make sure everyone is working productively, and perhaps take a quick oral reading record on the previous day's text with one of the students in the group.

Many teachers of young students like to bring everyone together at the end of each guided reading lesson for a whole-class activity before moving on to the next guided reading session.

Features of the Guided Reading Lesson for Emergent Readers

BEFORE READING
• Book introduction and comprehensive picture walk

DURING READING
• Teacher-led reading of text
• Individual reading of the text

AFTER READING
• Work with sounds, letters, and words
• Make your own book

Using manipulatives like *reading fingers* helps young readers with word-by-word tracking.

Before Reading

To introduce a new book to emergent readers, start by looking at the title and cover illustrations. You can provide a simple one sentence summary—"This is a book about…"—and a prompt or a question to activate prior knowledge.

I rarely have students talk about connections or predictions from the cover of the book because I've found, at this level, the dialogue can take off in directions totally unrelated to the book and cause confusion rather than activating schema. Then it's like herding cats to bring the students back to a focus on the book. For example, the book *A Sun, A Flower,* described in the sample lesson, has a picture of a sunflower on the cover. Letting the students free-associate about growing sunflowers, spitting sunflower seeds, and how hot the sun is will do little to help them navigate this book about compound words!

The book introduction for emergent readers is heavily scaffolded. As I hold the book, we "walk" through the book, page by page, discussing what we see in each picture, until we've gone through the entire book. During this *pic flic*, I can make sure students understand the structure and language patterns of the book, model directionality, discuss concepts, and introduce vocabulary that might be unfamiliar. For example, one book had the word *glove.* My students read the picture and said "mitt"; they needed to be taught that the word "glove" refers to a special kind of mitt with fingers in it and starts with letter *g.*

During Reading

After the picture walk, distribute the books so each student has his/her own copy. Give the students *reading fingers* (toy witch fingers from the Halloween section of the dollar store) to encourage them to track the print word by word. Give them a few moments to savor the feeling of the books and to flip through the pictures, then guide them as you read the text together several times.

Depending on the text and the group, you might read each page first, then have students "echo read" it after you. Or you can dive right in and read each page in chorus. Either way, the first reading is going to be a shared reading experience, led by the teacher. Remember that emergent readers can't yet process print independently. They "read" from memory and pictures, so they have to memorize the text through many exposures to it. As students develop decoding strategies, they will be able to negotiate the print on their own after the book introduction but, for now, we need to provide the initial support of reading together.

Only when you are confident that all students know what is on every page should students be asked to read their books individually. This process is made challenging by the fact that emergent readers can't read silently. They need to hear their own voices in order to know what they're reading. One way to prevent students from reading in chorus is to stagger their starting points. For example, I might say, "Jessica and Sunil, would you please start reading in a whisper voice. Everyone else, find your favorite picture in this book." When Jessica and Sunil have progressed a few pages into the book, I'll ask Thanh and Hayden to start, and if there are more students waiting, I might suggest that they hunt in the book for a letter that is in their name or a word that they know how to read until it is their turn to start.

I always remind students, demonstrating with my own book, "When you come to the end of the book, just close it up and go back to the beginning and read it again. See how many times you can read the *whole book* before I tell you to stop!"

Emergent readers need to hear their own voices in order to know what they are reading, so reading time can sometimes turn into a cacophony! Some ways to encourage students to read independently rather than joining with another reader:

- providing reading phones made from an elbow of PVC pipe
- staggering the starts so that students are reading at different places at any given time
- practicing whisper reading

While students are reading, listen to one at a time for a few seconds, providing individual prompting as needed. Because students learn to keep rereading the text until they are told to stop, they are getting plenty of practice with each text.

After Reading

The difference between this routine and round-robin reading is that this is purposeful and practiced—for both readers and listeners.

When I'm satisfied that everyone has read the text a few times, I'll stop the reading and perhaps take a minute to reinforce strategies: "You know, I saw Thanh look at the picture while he was reading to help him figure out the word. Looking at the picture is a great strategy that readers use to help them figure out the words." I might draw attention to holding the book the right way, tracking with a reading finger, or sounding out a letter. One way to practice oral reading is by inviting everyone to take a turn reading his or her favorite page to the group, then vote to see who else liked that page. You might talk about what you have read and do a retelling, but most emergent-level texts don't have a lot of metacognitive meat to chew on. There's little meaningful discussion arising out of a text that reads, for example, "The pigs, the ducks, the horse, the cows, the sheep, the chickens, the cows, the farm." But now that the students have memorized this text, you can go back into it to work with letters, words, and other print features.

Text matching and word- or letter-hunting are regular routines for emergent-level guided reading. Send students back into the book to hunt for words, letters, and patterns embedded in the text. Keep on hand a variety of pointers, framers, reading glasses, and other manipulatives to engage children as they revisit the text. (See page 162, Tips for Reading Manipulatives.) One day, students might be reading detectives with magnifying glasses; another day, they might be framing "glittering words" with a star-shaped swizzle stick.

As much as possible, link the word study to the text, but don't rule out playing sound games, sorting words or pictures by sound, practicing name writing, or chanting letters on the alphabet arc, if these activities meet the needs of the students in the group. A number of ideas for working with picture sorts, alphabet mats, and other games are provided in this chapter.

Must-Do

You might decide to take advantage of the small-group setting to do some interactive writing. In an interactive writing routine, you and students compose the text together—the students take turns doing the writing, with lots of teacher support and scaffolding.

My favorite must-do for emergent readers is to have them make their own books, following the pattern of the guided-reading text (this process is described on page 43). Sometimes I provide a framework for the students to complete and sometimes they do the writing entirely themselves. Other must-do activities for

After reading, students put the guided-reading text into their individual book boxes, where it is available for free-choice reading. One way to get students to reread them is to put a large sticky note in the back of each text. Have students "get an autograph" from everyone they read it to!

emergent readers include picture sorting, word and letter hunts, and alphabet games.

The guided reading sequence for emergent readers generally extends over two days. Emergent-level texts rarely merit more time than this, and you want to expose emerging readers to as many books as possible. At the end of the second day, the students add the book to their book boxes (and return one of the older guided-reading texts from their box), where they can keep it for free-choice reading.

Sample Areas of Focus

Once we thought that there was a magical moment of "readiness" when children suddenly became readers. Now we know that literacy begins to emerge as soon as children recognize the label on the toothpaste tube, the golden arches that identify a fast-food chain, or the red sign that tells Mom to stop the car.

Some reading professionals have argued about whether students are ready for guided reading at this stage of reading development. I confess that I have not always been comfortable with the idea of guided reading in Kindergarten. But when I came to accept that guided reading looks a little different in Kindergarten than at any other stage of reading development, I realized that there was much to be gained by pulling small groups of children together to work on sounds, letters, words, and books.

Most emergent readers have already learned that listening to books being read aloud can be an enjoyable and interesting experience. We want them to maintain that motivation as they begin to negotiate print. We also know that a strong foundation in oral language—both vocabulary and syntax—is essential for learning to read. After all, unlike mature readers, beginning readers can't read words they don't know! So we'd better make sure they know a lot of words.

Pre-literacy learnings directly correlated with future success in learning to read:
- phonemic awareness: the ability to hear the discrete sounds in words and to blend and segment those sounds for decoding and spelling
- concepts about print: the fundamental understandings readers have about approaching print, from directionality to word boundaries
- letter-name recognition: in random order, with speed and automaticity
- the alphabetic principle: the concept that letters represent sounds; and phonics: the guidelines that govern how those letters and sounds go together
- the ability to recognize and write one's own name.

(National Early Literacy Panel, 2010)

These understandings are incorporated into every aspect of the literacy program, but small-group instruction is an ideal time to reinforce and practice them. It's critical, of course, for emergent readers/writers to learn the alphabet letters and sounds, but reading is much more than just letter–sound correspondence. In the emergent-level guided reading sequence, we focus on three broad areas of guided-reading goals: working with sounds; working with letters and words; and working with books. Ideally, the three are integrated, with letters, words, and sounds connected to the guided-reading text. But there will be times that we work on letter-naming or name-writing in the small group, depending on the student's specific needs.

Working with Sounds

- Counting, pronouncing, blending, and segmenting syllables in spoken words
- Hearing and generating rhymes
- Identifying and matching initial and final sounds in words or picture names
- Identifying and matching long and short vowel sounds in words or picture names
- Isolating initial, medial, and final sounds (phonemes) in simple words
- Deleting, adding, or substituting sounds in one-syllable words to make new words

Working with Letters and Words

- Automatic recognition of upper- and lower-case letters by name, in random order
- Identifying specific letters
- Matching letters in different cases (upper and lower), fonts, sizes, etc.
- Identifying individual letters embedded in words
- Matching letters to the sounds they represent
- Identifying initial, final, and medial sounds in words read
- Generating other words with same sounds
- Spelling phonetically
- Recognizing and writing own name
- Recognizing and writing a few high-frequency words

Working with Books

- Identifying the parts of a book: front, back, cover, title, pictures, print
- Understanding directionality, such as where to start reading, left to right, return sweep, page turn
- Voice-print matching: tracking word by word
- Matching letters, words, and phrases
- Isolating given words and letters embedded in text
- Knowing that words have spaces around them
- Using pictures, context, and language patterns to "read" a book
- Telling what they have read
- Offering a personal response to reading (e.g., favorite part)

Lesson Routines

Working with Sounds

Phonemic awareness refers to the ability to hear and manipulate phonemes, the smallest units of sound in a word, such as individual letter sounds, blends, or digraphs. *Phonological awareness* is a more inclusive term that encompasses phonemes as well as larger units of sound, such as syllables and rimes.

Phonemic awareness has been closely correlated to reading success. Small-group instruction provides an ideal opportunity to support and extend children's ability to hear syllables, rhymes, and individual sounds, then to manipulate those sounds in reading. At its most basic, phonological awareness involves the ability to hear and count syllables and to recognize and generate rhymes. We also want students to be able to identify initial, final, and medial sounds, leading to blending words for decoding and segmenting words for writing. At its most sophisticated, phonemic awareness skills include isolating, deleting, and replacing phonemes in words, such as *cart* to *art* to *mart* to *march*.

Phonemic awareness instruction should take only a few of the 18 minutes of small-group instruction, and only as needed by the students. The National Reading Panel in the U.S., in its meta-analysis of the research on reading instruction, reported that the most effective phonemic awareness programs occupied between 5 and 18 hours in the entire year. Even at the upper limit, that is no more than 6 minutes a day, or 30 minutes a week. Most children develop phonemic awareness easily and naturally just from living in a world of language. In fact, at least 80% of children develop phonemic awareness without any explicit instruction at all (IRA/NAEYC, 1998). Reading books together, reciting rhymes, and singing songs all help to develop phonemic awareness by drawing children's attention to the sounds of language in the world around them.

Picture Sorts

Learning Goal: Students will be able to match pictures with common sounds.

It's easy to use clipart to create picture cards for sorting, but there are many websites that have this done already, including: www.carlscorner.us.com/Sorts.htm and www.fcrr.org

Gather a collection of small objects or clipart pictures for students to sort. If possible, laminate the picture cards for durability and reuse. Remember that these activities focus only on sounds, not words and letters, so work with pictures and small objects rather than letters.

There are two types of sorts. Open sorts are activities in which the students create their own criteria for sorting. Closed sorts are activities in which students are given specific criteria for sorting; for example, students can be asked to sort by

- number of syllables
- rhymes
- initial or final consonant sound
- medial vowel sound

You might want to create sorting mats. For example, a plastic placemat can be divided into two, three, or four boxes, using heavy marker. An alternative is to put small pieces of magnetic tape on the back of each picture so students can sort them onto a metal tray (such as a cookie sheet) divided into sections with masking tape.

As you conduct this activity, require students to tell why they are putting a particular picture in a particular column. For example, "This is a star. *Star* rhymes with *car*, so it goes here with the car."

Must-Do

If you need to have some kind of product for accountability, have students glue the picture cards onto the sorting board (but take into account that gluing eats up time that could be spent thinking and reading). Otherwise, have students work in pairs to sort the pictures and articulate the reasons for their actions. Working in pairs on these tasks generates more discussion and enables peers to assess and correct one another. Start with two categories (particular sounds, rhymes, or syllables you've worked on during the lesson). Later, students can learn to sort sounds into more than two categories.

Syllable Segmenting

Learning Goal: Students will be able to identify, pronounce, blend, and segment syllables in spoken words.

Work with students' names and other key words from the guided reading text to listen for syllables.

- Say the words and distinctly separate them into syllables (e.g., *Jess–i–ca; An–drew*).
- Have students clap, snap, march, or do another action for each syllable in given words and students' names. Clap and count the syllables as you read them (e.g., "*Jess–i–ca / 1, 2, 3*").
- Have students compare the syllables in words. Which words have the same number of syllables? Which words have the most syllables?
- Use a collection of small objects, such as a pencil, eraser, glasses. Have students sort the items according to the number of syllables.
- Syllable riddles: Invite students to generate words with a specified number of syllables. (Who has a name with two syllables? What is a yellow fruit with three syllables?)

Must-Do

Have students work independently or in partners to sort a collection of pictures or small objects by number of syllables.

Train Sounds

Learning Goal: Students will be able to identify initial and final sounds (phonemes) in one-syllable words.

Sound boxes, or Elkonin boxes, are an effective tool for helping children learn to hear sounds in words, to segment words, to sequence sounds, and to connect sounds to letters. This process involves sliding a marker into a row of boxes drawn on a page, one box for each sound that is heard in a word.

Instead of markers, I use magnetic train cars to reinforce beginning (engine) sounds, medial (boxcar) sounds, and ending (caboose) sounds in a word. For example, for the word *pig*, we will say /p/ as we move the engine, /i/ as we move the boxcar, and /g/ as we move the caboose. We can even "couple" the cars to blend the sounds in a word; we can separate them to segment the sounds.

Must-Do

Provide a set of picture cards for students to sort by initial, medial, or final sound.

The Sound Bus

Learning Goal: Students will be able to identify initial and final sounds (phonemes) in one-syllable words.

Use a picture of a schoolbus or a toy schoolbus in this game. A given word is on the bus, and sounds hop off and on the bus to create new words. For example, if the word *star* is on the bus, the /s/ sound might hop off the bus to create *tar*. Or the /t/ sound might hop on the back of the bus to create *start*. If /st/ hopped off the bus, it would leave *art*. And if /c/ hopped on the front of the bus, it would make *cart*.

Must-Do

Sound manipulation like this is a very sophisticated skill and most students will not master it until they are reading conventionally. It is more appropriate in a teacher-guided setting than as an independent-learning must-do.

More Games for Playing with Sounds

These games can be taught and practiced in small-group instruction, then used for must-do practice independently.

Snap!

This traditional card game can be adapted to use picture cards for phonological awareness. Students divide the deck of picture cards in two and each player has a stack of cards. Both players flip the top card face-up at the same time. If the two face-up cards don't rhyme (have the same beginning sound, number of syllables, etc.), players flip over another card on top of the previous one. (It might be necessary to teach the students to count together, "1, 2, 3, flip!" to ensure that they flip their cards at the same time.) Players keep flipping cards until they get a rhyming pair and they shout "Snap!" The first player to shout "Snap!" gets to pick up both piles of face-up cards. If there's a tie, each player takes his or her own pile of cards back.

The Oddball Game

A rubber ball with a silly face on it stands for oddball words—words that don't belong with the others. Just as the oddball doesn't belong with the other balls, there are oddball words that don't fit with the other words in a group. For example, in the set of words *sing, ring, fling*, and *book,* the oddball word is *book* because it doesn't rhyme with the others. Start with very obvious examples and move to more subtle examples, like *sing, ring, fling, song.* Roll the ball to a player; the player holding the ball has to tell which word is the oddball.

The oddball game can be played with beginning or ending sounds, rhyming words, vowel sounds, etc.

I Hear with My Little Ear

This game is a variation on I Spy, but with clues given for the sounds of words. For example, "I hear with my little ear a word that means something you wear on your feet that starts with /sh/."

Simon Says

The leader says a pair of words. If they rhyme/have the same sound/have the same number of syllables/etc., the players must do a designated action, such as putting their hands on their heads, plugging their noses, closing their eyes, etc.

Working with Letters and Words

Rapid automatic naming (RAN) of alphabet letters is considered to be a strong predictor of reading success. It's important for students to know the sounds represented by the letters, but knowing letter names provides a working language for talking about the symbols we use to read and write. And, in truth, 22 of the 26 letters of the alphabet have their sounds in their names. Of course, we also want students to be able to connect the letters to their sounds in special ways to form (or decode) words. As children begin to grasp the connection between letters and sounds, they can start blending sounds for reading and segmenting sounds for writing.

The National Reading Panel in the U.S. determined that systematic phonics instruction (instruction that introduces letter–sound correspondences in a predetermined sequence) is most effective in Kindergarten and Grade 1. Beyond first grade, phonics instruction has not been found to contribute to spelling or reading comprehension. That's because K–1 is pretty much the only age group that has a larger speaking than writing vocabulary. When a Kindergartener "sounds out" a word when reading, it's likely that he/she will recognize that word; when a third grader needs to sound out an unfamiliar word, there's a good chance that he/she won't know what it means. No single approach to phonics instruction has been found to be superior to any other (NICHD, 2000), but programs that focus too much on letters and sounds out of context, and not enough on putting them to use, are unlikely to be very effective. Phonics is not an end in itself; it is a tool for reading and writing.

Alphabet Mats

Learning Goal: Students will be able to name individual alphabet letters automatically.

Create or purchase a laminated mat with the alphabet letters in upper and lower case, displayed in a row or as an arc. They can be used in small-group instruction to support identifying names and sounds of alphabet letters. Some alphabet mat activities:

- Follow the reader: Echo-read the alphabet, with the teacher or a student as leader. Have someone draw a random letter from a letter bag and start from that letter.
- As you point to the letters, sing them to a familiar tune (not the traditional alphabet song). Do a rhythmical action such as snap-clap as you read the letters. Establishing a rhythm helps avoid the runaway-train phenomenon in group reading.
- Use different voices to read the letters. Alternate high squeaky voices with low soft voices.
- Read the alphabet backward or read every second letter.
- Take turns reading (e.g., boys and girls, individual students). Have each turn read two or three letters at a time.
- If you have a colored alphabet mat, read only the letters in one color.
- Show Me: e.g., "Show me a *T*." Have students take turns saying the "show me."
- Pinky Point (like Simon Says): e.g., "Pinky point to *L*" (point with the little finger).
- Match plastic alphabet letters or letter cards drawn at random with letters on the mat.
- Have students point out letters that come before or after a designated letter: e.g., What letter comes before *X*? What letter comes after *G*?

Alphabet arc templates may be downloaded from a number of sources, including: http://communication4all.co.uk/Classroom%20Basics/Rainbow%20Arc%202.pdf and http://www.alphabetmats.com/matfront.html

Must-Do

Students practice reading the alphabet arc in pairs, matching letters on the alphabet mat with plastic letters or tiles, or taking turns drawing letter tiles from a bag and seeing who can be first to find the letter on their alphabet mat.

Letter Bags

Learning Goal: Students will be able to name random alphabet letters and sounds automatically.

Provide each student with a bag containing all the letters of the alphabet or a designated set, depending on the lesson focus. (Consider whether you want all capitals, all lower case, or a mixture.) Play games for identifying, naming, and sorting the letters and their sounds.

- Have students take turns reaching into their bags, grabbing a letter, and, without looking, trying to name it by its shape. If they are right, they keep the letter; if not, they throw the letter back in the bag.
- In Letter Bag Bingo, students choose four letters at random from their bags. You call out a letter (or letter-sound). If a student has the letter, he/she places it on top of the corresponding letter on his/her alphabet mat. The first student to place all his or her letters is the winner. Gradually increase the number of letters drawn.

Must-Do

Students can engage in the same activities independently as in the guided reading lesson. For example, prepare Bingo cards with sets of random letters. Have students work in pairs to take turns drawing letters from their letter bags. If a player has that letter, he/she marks it on his/her Bingo card. The first person to get a row of letters covered calls "Bingo!" and wins.

Name Games

Learning Goal: Students will be able to read and write their own names.

Emergent readers typically recognize and label the letters of their own names before any other letters of the alphabet. Name writing teaches students to explore print, to use symbols to represent ideas, to connect those symbols to sounds, to combine letters into words, and to see words as separate entities. Small-group reading provides an excellent opportunity to support students as they learn to print their own names and compare the letters in their names with other names.

Take time to point out the difference between capital and lower-case letters. Provide students with a letter bag with the letters in their own names to "mix and fix." Have students use a sorting mat with a set of alphabet letters to sort the letters in their names and not in their names. Compare which letters appear in more than one name in the group. Sort names by syllables or letters.

Have students practice printing the letters in their names in the air, by tracing on a table, by using markers on a whiteboard, or by using pencil or marker on paper. When children can approximate the printing of their own names, work on more-accurate letter formation.

Must-Do

- Must-do activities for independent learning include working in pairs to have students compare alphabet letters in both names, letters in one name but not the other, letters in neither name.
- Give students practice printing their own names with rainbow writing. Students trace over their own name with different colored markers or crayons.

Letter–Sound Games

Learning Goal: Students will be able to make a connection between letters and the sounds they represent, and begin to use letter–sound correspondence for decoding and spelling.

Many of the same routines used for letters and sounds separately can be used for letter–sound correspondence as well. For example, use the alphabet mat to read the alphabet by the sounds of the letters rather than the names. See chapter 4: Early Readers, for more ideas about decoding and invented spelling (i.e., "bubblegum writing").

Working with Books

Isolated practice in letters, sounds, and words is of little value unless there is application to connected reading. This is why guided reading is so important, even for emergent readers. Children learn to apply what they know about letters and sound to negotiating real print in appropriately challenging texts. Book work is an opportunity to reinforce concepts about print: distinguishing the front of the book from the back, rightside-up from upside-down, print from pictures. Only through working with books can children learn about word boundaries, as they track during reading and isolate individual words within the text. Book work provides opportunities to match isolated lines, words, and letters with those embedded in connected text and to use visual (print and pictures) cues as well as syntax and meaning to identify individual words.

Show What You Know

Learning Goal: Students will be able to identify known print features.

This before-reading activity teaches students to activate prior knowledge by identifying known print and visual features of a book from its cover. Introduce a new guided-reading text by showing students the cover and inviting them to "show what they know" before telling them the title or anything about the book. Students might point out features of the picture, as well as identifying elements of the print, from individual letters to complete words.

Must-Do

We want students to develop the habit of perusing the cover information when they read independently, but there is no formal must-do associated with this lesson.

Parts of a Book

Learning Goal: Students will be able to identify the front and back covers, title, author/illustrator, and "birthday" of a book.

Some students will not be able to identify the parts of a book, and others will know the concepts but not vocabulary, such as *author*, *illustrator*, and *title*. Take time during the book introduction to identify each part of the book, including the copyright ("birthday"), if it's indicated in the book. Take time to talk about the purpose of each part and why it's important for readers to know about them.

Must-Do

This lesson does not have a must-do component, but looking for the author, illustrator, and copyright is a good habit for readers to form.

Spaces around Words

Learning Goal: Students will be able to match individual spoken words with words in print.

Understanding the concept of word boundaries is an important but difficult step on the road to reading. After all, we rarely speak in individual words; we speak in streams of words. It's hard to hear individual words in speech and it's hard to understand that words are separated by spaces in print.

I've found that it helps to identify the spaces between words. Some teachers use "spaceman" markers to separate words in writing. The same tool may be used to identify the spaces in reading. We often *finger frame* words in reading, saying, "Space to space, there's a word."

Provide each student with a "reading finger" (a toy finger to place over the reader's own finger) to stress tracking word by word. Chopsticks or other pointers can also be used. See Appendix page 162 for more ideas for reading manipulatives.

Must-Do

Encourage students to use reading fingers or other tools to track words when reading independently.

Print Matching

Learning Goal: Students will be able to match words in the text with words in isolation.

When we match words in guided reading, we are teaching students to look for print features of those words, and we are also reinforcing the concept that words have boundaries. Start by providing students with entire lines of text for them to match with text in the book, then move to phrases, and finally to individual words.

Must-Do

Provide students with a cut-up copy of the text, with print and pictures separated, for them to match the print to the pictures.

Make Your Own Book

Learning Goal: Students will be able to create books based on the pattern or framework from a guided-reading text.

This sample was created by a Kindergarten student after reading a book called *Dear Santa*.

Because emergent-level guided-reading texts are heavily patterned, it's easy to create new books following the same structure, and this is a wonderful follow-up to reading. Use the shared- or interactive-writing component of the guided reading lesson to model writing from a sentence stem or framework based on the pattern of the guided-reading text.

Must-Do

Have students use the same sentence stem or similar ones to create their own books. I like to make several sheets of paper available, so that students can make their books as long as they choose. (Why would we ever limit our students to just one page?) When the pages are complete, the students can staple them together into a book. We often add an autograph page at the end, for students to get a signature from everyone who listens to them read this book. The book is added to their book boxes as a text for independent reading.

The Reading–Writing Connection

Emergent readers are role-play writers as well as readers. They tell stories through pictures, sometimes adding scribbles, random letters, or letter-like symbols as "writing" (see sample in margin). Until they begin consistently making letter–sound connections, they are not ready for invented (phonetic) spelling. This is an excellent time to demonstrate what their talk looks like in print, through shared- and interactive-writing experiences.

Readers at this stage	*Writers at this stage*
• use letters, words, and pictures to get information from books	• use letters, words, and pictures to gather and convey ideas
• have mastered most concepts about print, including directionality and distinguishing pictures from print	• begin to write in lines from left to right, top to bottom
• begin to understand spaces around words	• begin to understand spaces around words
• connect letters and sounds to decode during reading	• connect letters and sounds to spell during writing
• read some high-frequency words automatically	• write some high-frequency words conventionally
• begin to understand sentences as groups of words with punctuation	• begin to write sentences with capitals and punctuation
• prefer to read topics relating to their personal experience	• prefer to write about topics relating to their personal experience
• move beyond patterned text	• coordinate pictures and print on the page

Readers at this stage	Writers at this stage
• can cope with more than one line on a page • can retell what was read	• can relate to more than one detail in writing • will try to write most words in speaking vocabulary

Shared Writing

Beginning readers/writers benefit from seeing their own words in print, a practice also known as shared writing or language experience. Using the guided-reading text as a springboard, work with students to generate word lists or sentences. Record students' ideas, thinking aloud about the process, such as what letters to use, whether to use a capital or lower-case letter, where to leave spaces, etc.

I like to use the "buzz book" approach developed by Texas Kindergarten teachers Bonnie Jackson and Shelley Vaughn (www.thekcrew.net). I introduce a prompt related to the guided-reading text or the focus word study, then give students a couple of minutes to "buzz" with a partner to respond. Together, we compose the response—a sentence or a group of words—interactively, with students taking turns writing letters and words while I support and guide. The advantage of the "buzz" is to give all students an opportunity to participate through talk.

Cut-Up Sentences

Cut-up sentences are a good small-group routine. Together, compose a sentence about what was read, which you record on a piece of paper, making sure to exaggerate the spaces between words. Count the words on your fingers and, as you write, think aloud about word and letter features (e.g., double letters, beginning sounds, etc.). Then provide each student with a copy of the sentence, for them to cut apart (good practice for word boundaries) and reassemble on another piece of paper. Some teachers have students copy the sentence themselves, but I haven't found that copying a sentence offers enough learning to be worth the time expended.

With a small group of students, it's possible to have every student generate his or her own sentence in shared writing (see sample in margin). This collection of sentences serves as a shared reading text, giving an opportunity to revisit letters and other print concepts (e.g., capitals and periods). Each student then has his/her own sentence to cut up and reassemble (i.e., mix and fix), then illustrate. These sentences might be compiled into a group booklet for independent reading.

Writing with Pictures

At this stage, students can be given opportunities to draw and describe pictures that retell a story, describe a favorite part, or extend the experience with reading. For example, using the example of *The Farm*, described earlier, they might draw farm animals that might be added to the book. At first, you might record the student's caption for the picture; as the children learn the alphabet, they can be encouraged to label their own pictures with letters and words.

I can
I can teach. (Miss S.)
I can run. (Vanessa)
I can swim. (Shaira)
I can run. (Josue)
I can have friends. (Hailee)
I can play. (Yulicia)
I can learn my words. (Jonae)
I can see. (Carlos)
I can play. (Taliyah)
I can have fun. (Teyanni)
I can have friends. (Ja'various)
I can play with my friends. (Kaliel)
I can swim. (Yomar)
I can play football (Joshua)

Sample Guided Reading Lesson Plan for Emergent Readers

Group: Level B

Title	**Learning Goals**
A Sun, A Flower	Text Level: using picture cues Tracking and directionality Compound Words Word Level: Letter recognition/matching Beginning and ending sounds

Text/Book Introduction

Preview:

This is a book all about compound words. Just take a look at the cover of the book. What do you see? A sunflower. What two little words went together to make the word sunflower?

    Picture walk through the entire book to model the directionality and introduce all the vocabulary.

    Distribute the books and reading fingers for tracking. Read the text together chorally before having the students read on their own.

Prior Knowledge:

We've been talking about special kinds of words called compound words that are formed when you put two little words together, like class *and* room *to form* classroom *or* mail *and* box *to form…? Can anyone remember any other words that are made of two little words?*

Purpose:

Now it's your turn to read the whole book on your own. When you come to the end of the book, just flip right back to the front and read it again. See how many times you can read the whole book before I tell you to stop. And when I tap your book like this, will you read for me, please?

Day 1	**Must-Do**
• Book introduction and picture walk. • Read the text together chorally. • Students read independently, tracking with their reading fingers. • *Everyone find your favorite page to read aloud.*	• Buddy-read the whole text again, taking turns page by page. • Provide each student with a cut-up version of the text and have them match the pictures and the words.
Day 2	**Must-Do**
• Reread text independently. • Hold up picture cards for students to match. • Hold up word cards for students to match. • Letter/word hunt detectives: Who can find a word that starts with *b*? Who can find a word that ends with *s*? • Brainstorm compound words.	• Make your own compound word book.

4

Guiding Early Readers

Jacob is in deep concentration with his head bent over a book. With his finger pointing to the text, he calls out each word. From time to time, he pauses and can be heard sounding out a word letter by letter. Occasionally Jacob reads a word incorrectly, but often he keeps on reading anyway. Jacob knows how to connect letters and sounds to figure out words, but sometimes he sacrifices meaning for visual cues. He can hold on to several details in his head and can retell a story in sequence after he has read it. Jacob sees himself as a reader and enjoys having lots of books in his book box.

When children have mastered basic concepts about print and can connect letters with sounds, we consider them to be early readers. This occurs, for most children, between mid-Kindergarten and well into Grade 1. The ability to decode—to use the phonetic principle to solve words—is probably the key indicator of the early-reading stage, and it is the start of what many would consider to be real reading work. Early readers like Jacob are unable to read silently; they need to hear what they read in order to understand it. As readers progress through this stage, they begin to take an interest in reading texts with multiple characters and a basic storyline, but still prefer familiar topics that connect to their own lives and experiences.

   One of the problems of early decoders is that sometimes meaning is sacrificed as the reader attends to the visual features of the word. I recall my own daughter at that stage making a particularly egregious miscue. When I asked her, "Jennifer, does that make sense?" she replied incredulously, "You mean it's all supposed to make sense?" The big challenge for early readers is to ensure that their reading must always make sense, first and foremost, but also to match the print on the page. For this, they must draw on three main cueing systems: semantic (meaning), syntactic (language structure), and phonetic (letter–sound correspondence).

Early Readers

- can identify most or all of the alphabet letters and sounds
- use phonics clues to solve words
- stretch out (segment) sounds to write words and blend sounds to read words
- use picture and text cues for word-solving
- have mastered most concepts about print, including voice–print matching
- track word-by-word during reading

- understand most phonological awareness concepts, from rhymes to blending and segmenting
- can cope with a storyline with more than one character
- return sweep for two or more lines of print
- retell the details of a story or nonfiction text in sequence, with prompting
- talk about their reading, articulating what they wonder and what they think
- read a repertoire of high-frequency words automatically
- express ideas in writing, using a combination of conventional and temporary spellings

Texts for Early Readers

Because early readers have a growing repertoire of words that they recognize automatically and are beginning use the phonetic principle to decode unfamiliar words, they no longer depend on predictable or heavily patterned text. They enjoy reading a simple storyline and start identifying the elements of a story: characters, setting, problem and solution. They can tolerate more print on the page, but still use illustrations as a comprehension aid. At the beginning of this stage, texts might have two or three lines of print on the page, but they gradually increase in length. Narrative text will often contain dialogue among two or more characters, with the accompanying punctuation. Informational text might include text features, such as a table of contents or labeled diagrams.

Once our early readers have mastered voice–print matching, we want to start weaning them off word-by-word tracking. A key feature of good early-level text is line breaks at meaningful phrases to support phrased reading. Other features of early level texts:

- fiction and nonfiction on topics familiar to young children
- simple storylines, sometimes with a twist or surprise ending
- generally 8–16 pages with somewhat enlarged print
- illustrations that support the storyline or facts
- simple sentences with appropriate punctuation
- two or three or more lines of print on the page
- mostly high-frequency and decodable words
- key vocabulary repeated and reinforced
- some unique text features, such as speech bubbles, labeled diagrams, headings

Baby Canada Goose Flies South by Janet Intscher, illustrated by Rebecca Buchanan (2001). Reprinted courtesy Curriculum Plus Publishing.

Baby Goose lived by a pond with his mother and father.

One day, Father Goose said, "It's fall now. The snow will come soon and we will fly south."

The Guided Reading Lesson for Early Readers

See page 66 for a sample guided reading lesson plan for early readers.

The guided reading lesson for early readers demands a greater degree of independence than the lesson for emergent readers. Early readers are expected to process most of the print on their own, so we don't read the text aloud for them. A good book introduction should provide the support they need to read the rest of the text with a manageable amount of reading work. During reading, students read the text independently (not chorally). Readers at this stage still need to hear themselves read, so most of the reading will be oral and individual. After reading, we generally focus on comprehension strategies, retelling, and big ideas before revisiting the text to focus on print features.

Before Reading

Don't take a picture walk on every page of the text for the early reader; remember, you want the students to negotiate most of the print themselves.

You can do a selective picture walk on pages that might present vocabulary or conceptual challenges to the readers and discuss those pages. This is a good time to teach the students to do their own picture walks as a preview for reading.

Remember that the vocabulary in early-level texts consists mostly of high-frequency and decodable words; unique vocabulary is reinforced several times throughout the text. Therefore, carefully consider whether or not to preteach this vocabulary. Here are some considerations:

- Is the word critical to understanding the rest of the text?
- Are there inadequate supports in the text for students to decode the word on their own?
- Will the word be useful for students to be able to know and use?

An easy review of high-frequency words can be done by presenting the word on a sentence strip, revealing one letter at a time, and inviting students to guess the word.

If the answer to these questions is yes, then it's worth spending the time to preteach that particular word. Often the word will already be in the students' speaking vocabularies; you just need to reinforce its print features for reading. You can provide magnetic letters and a small cookie sheet or metal stove-burner cover for each student, and guide them through a word-building activity: for example, for the story *All Clean*, we used letters to construct *an*, *can*, *clan*, *clean*, *cleaned*, *cleaning*, *cleaner*.

It's also a good idea to review any high-frequency words that appear in the text, both in context and in isolation. It's essential that students be able to read these words automatically.

Features of the Guided Reading Lesson for Early Readers

BEFORE READING
- Text introduction
- Individual picture walk

DURING READING
- Independent reading in phrases
- Comprehension focus; e.g., self-monitoring

AFTER READING
- Retelling
- Revisit the text to focus on print features
- Discussion for higher-level thinking

During Reading

With early readers, I find myself spending lots of time on the self-monitoring comprehension strategy. As they begin to focus their energy on decoding, it's not uncommon for early readers to sacrifice meaning for matching sounds. They often read words that look vaguely right, but don't self-correct even if those words don't make sense. Readers at this stage must develop the habit of using all their cueing systems: meaning and syntax as well as visual.

Early readers are still reading orally, so stagger start the reading, just as with emergent readers. Once students have mastered voice–print matching, begin to wean them off word-by-word tracking and encourage phrased reading. Replacing reading fingers with sliders (rulers) to slide under each line of text helps young readers think and read in groups of words rather than word by word.

As always, listen in on the students, one by one, as they read from their own texts. If you anticipate particular trouble spots, ask a student to go back and reread that page so you can see how well he/she has coped with the challenge.

After Reading

After reading, we often revisit any trouble spots to discuss the ways in which students monitored and self-corrected; I might say, "I noticed that Joey read the word *cage* as *cape*, but then he realized that it didn't make sense in the story and he went back and looked at the end of the word." Invite students to share their own experiences; say something like "Jessica, tell the other boys and girls what strategies you used when you came to that word *feather* and didn't know what it said." These conversations send crucial messages: most importantly, that reading must make sense; and that when reading doesn't make sense, readers need to stop and use their strategies to "fix up their mix-ups."

Retelling is an important after-reading focus at this stage. When students retell what they have read, look for them to provide all the key details, relay those details in the correct sequence, and use key words from the text. The small-group guided reading lesson is an excellent opportunity to provide students with plenty of practice in retelling; however, retelling addresses only the surface ideas of the text. To encourage students to respond more deeply to text, we need to stimulate their thinking through big-idea questions and prompts.

At this stage, however, most of the readers' energy is still devoted to processing individual words. On subsequent rereadings in the guided-reading sequence, focus on word-level comprehension by hunting for word and letter features in the text, then analyzing the words collected. Readers at this stage have mastered most individual consonant sounds and many vowel sounds, so working with letter patterns is an important focus. As much as possible, use a whole-to-part-to-whole structure for word study, beginning and ending with reading connected text, with any isolated word work in between.

After reading, students place the guided-reading text into their book boxes to use for independent reading. Like emergent readers, early readers can be encouraged to reread the text if you insert a large sticky note in the back of the book for collecting "autographs" from everyone they read the book to.

Sample Areas of Focus

It's important to increase early readers' reading stamina for longer texts, requiring them to hold more information in their heads as they read. We want them to learn to "talk to their brains" about their reading, asking themselves questions and monitoring their own comprehension. We want early readers to develop their ability to use the phonetic principle—letter–sound relationships—to read across entire words rather than relying on just the beginning and ending sounds. In addition to reviewing individual letters, we work on letter patterns: blends, digraphs, vowel combinations, and rimes.

Because the foundation of comprehension is retelling, we want students to be able to recognize key details and relate them in sequence, to identify structural elements, such as characters, setting, problem and solution. Texts at this stage do not always have a lot of layers of inference but, with guiding questions and prompting, we can encourage students to think more deeply about what they

Readers at this stage must develop the habit of using all their cueing systems: meaning, syntactical, and visual.

Retelling can support both comprehension and assessment, but we need to teach students what they are expected to do in a retell.

49

read, to make connections to their background knowledge and experience, and to see the relationship between what they wonder as readers and what they think or know from the reading.

Demonstrating Comprehension of Text

- Previewing text to prepare for reading
- Retelling all key details in sequence
- Identifying story structure: characters, setting, problem, solution
- Identifying and describing characters
- Recognizing and using basic nonfiction text features, such as headings, captions, labels
- Connecting to prior knowledge before, during, and after reading
- Questioning (wondering) during reading
- Self-talk for monitoring comprehension and clarification
- Guided inference, evaluation, and prediction
- Contributing to prompted discussion of big ideas
- Distinguishing informational reading from story reading
- Identifying time-order words, such as *first, next, later*, etc., and how they affect sequence of events
- Recognizing unique vocabulary, such as size words, sensory descriptions, vivid verbs, synonyms for "said," etc.
- Noting relationships between illustrations and text

Applying Letter Knowledge and Word-Solving Strategies

- Identifying and using long and short vowel combinations
- Identifying inflectional endings: *-s, -ed, -ing*
- Decoding one-syllable words by segmenting sounds
- Writing one-syllable words by blending sounds
- Decoding two-syllable words by breaking them into syllables
- Working with consonant combinations such as digraphs (e.g., *th, sh, wh*) and blends (e.g., *bl, cr, fl, str, sk, sp*)
- Identifying and using basic rimes and onsets for word-solving and spelling
- Manipulating phoneme sounds in words, especially vowels (*cub/cube; stop/step*)
- Integrating meaning, syntax, and phonics for solving challenging words

Reading with Increasing Fluency

- Automatic recognition of high-frequency words
- Moving from word-by-word tracking to reading in phrases
- Using appropriate expression, especially for dialogue

Responding to Reading

- Participating in guided discussion after reading
- Expressing personal thoughts and feelings about what was read and identifying favorite parts
- Writing text innovations using patterns and ideas from reading
- Drawing pictures to retell or extend a story

Lesson Routines

Comprehension of Text

Do-It-Yourself Picture Walk

Learning Goal: Students will be able to prepare for reading by previewing pictures.

Before a read-aloud or other reading experience, teachers often guide students in a picture walk to preview the text, activate prior knowledge, invite predictions, introduce new vocabulary, and set the tone for the reading. However, it's also a good strategy for students to use independently as they prepare for reading.

A picture walk (also known as a pic-flic) is a quick flip through the illustrations in a text to establish a context for the reading. As we peruse the pictures, we think about the answers to questions of who, what, where, why, and when. This routine can also raise some questions in the reader's mind—questions that the text might answer. Tell students that one way we get our brains ready to read is by flipping quickly through the pictures in the book and talking to our brains about what we see in the pictures. Using a new guided-reading text, walk through the first few pages, covering the print and prompting students to talk with their partners about what they see in the pictures and what they predict the story will be about. After a few pages of guidance, have students work in pairs to flip through their own books and talk to their partners about what they see. Invite students to share their predictions and questions before returning to the book to read the print.

Must-Do

Provide students with an unfamiliar text and have them work in partners to do a pic-flic in preparation for the next day's guided-reading session. At the next lesson, talk about their ideas from the pictures before introducing the new text.

Making Connections During Reading

Learning Goal: Students will be able to make connections between what they read and the experiences of their own lives.

One of the most important strategies we have for making sense of reading is to connect what we read to what we already know in our background knowledge. For many readers at all stages, failure to activate the appropriate background knowledge—or even a lack of background knowledge—can be a significant impediment to comprehension.

Teacher questioning, prompting, and probing can help students become aware of the automatic connections they make and can teach students to activate their existing background knowledge to help make sense of the reading. Invite connections before reading to get ready to read, during reading to make sense of the text, and after reading to extend knowledge and experience.

Pause during or after reading to invite students to respond to questions: *Does this character remind you of someone you know? Does anything in the book remind you of something that has happened to you?* When students come to a place in their reading that doesn't make sense, it can help to think about what the text reminds them of. Have students TTYN (Talk to Your Neighbor, see page 23) about the connections they have made during reading. Always BIBB (see page 24), or bring it back to the book, and discuss how this helps them understand the text.

Must-Do

Sketch and label a connections picture, using a piece of paper folded in half or the graphic organizer on page 67. On one half of the page, sketch and label an event or situation from the reading; on the other side, sketch and label a personal experience that connects to the event in the reading.

Wondering During Reading

Learning Goal: Students will be able to self-question during reading.

Good readers wonder all the time. They wonder what will happen next. They wonder what the character will do or why the character did what he/she did. They wonder what the author meant. Asking questions during reading helps us set a purpose for reading, focus our thinking, and monitor our own comprehension as we think about the clues the author gives us to answer our questions. Model and demonstrate wondering during a read-aloud or shared reading; guided reading is the opportunity for students to practice wondering as they negotiate print.

Before reading a guided-reading text, invite students to take a picture walk with their partners and to tell their partners what they are wondering as they look at the pictures. Tell students that the purpose for reading on this day is to think about what they are wondering. During reading, pause at a couple of strategic points and ask students to tell what they are wondering and what they think the answers to their "I wonders" might be. After reading, talk about whether their wonderings were answered in the story.

Must-Do

Have students read books of their choice to their buddies. They may, but don't need to, read from the same book. Teach them to use timers so each student takes a turn reading for one minute. At the end of one minute, the reader stops and the listening buddy tells the reader what he or she is wondering about the reading. Then the other partner has a turn to read from his or her own book for one minute and the listening buddy tells what he/she is wondering. Students continue taking turns until reading time is up.

Fix Up the Mix-ups

Learning Goal: Students will be able to monitor their own reading and make necessary corrections.

Remind students that every word they read should make sense, sound right, and match the print. Good readers make mistakes all the time. The important thing is to catch mistakes and fix up the mix-ups.

Take a few minutes to model self-monitoring for the students. Read a page from their guided-reading text aloud, make a deliberate miscue, and ask students to tell how they know this isn't the right word.

Tell students that, when they read, they need to use their eyes, their ears, and their heads. As they read to themselves, take turns listening in on individuals. During reading, prompt them if they miscue (after allowing time for them to self-correct). After reading, celebrate the strategy use you observed.

Teach students to ask themselves these questions as they read:
- Does my reading make sense?
- Does it sound right?
- Does it look right?

Must-Do

Have students buddy read, taking turns reading for one or two minutes at a time. At the end of each reading time, partners talk to each other about whether everything made sense, sounded right, and matched the print.

Signal Words that Tell Where or When

Learning Goal: Students will be able to identify prepositions that indicate place and time, and use them to support reading comprehension.

Remind students that drivers use signs around them to show where and when to turn, to go straight, to stop, or to go. Writers also use words as signals. Groups of words like *in the house* or *after school* tell where and when something is happening in the story.

After reading, have students revisit the text to hunt for phrases that tell where things happen. Create an anchor chart of where signals, such as *in, on, under, beside.* In another lesson, do the same for words that tell when things happen. This will include not only prepositions such as *after* and *before*, but also adverbs, such as *soon, later, suddenly*, etc.

Must-Do

Have students make their own signal-word picture dictionaries on a piece of paper divided in four. Students choose any four of the when or where signal words from the chart and illustrate each one.

Talk to Your Brain

Good readers talk to themselves in their heads as they read. I like to call this "talking to your brain." In this lesson, student practice talking aloud about what they wonder, what they think, and what connections they make to the text. Then they apply this by talking to themselves when they read independently.

Plan stopping points in the text where students will think about their thinking and share it with a partner. Have students read to a predetermined point in the text (or revisit a particular section of text that has already been read). Give them a moment to generate a wondering, a thought, or a connection, then ask them to share their thinking with their partners.

Must-Do

Because this routine is directly related to the guided-reading process, no must-do is specifically designated. However, we want to encourage readers to always talk their brains during reading.

Retelling Activities

Retelling is a proven way of supporting and assessing comprehension. In a retell, students are expected to recount every key detail in the order they occurred in the story. They also try to use as many vocabulary words from the story as possible.

There are a number of ways we can support retelling as part of the guided-reading program. Sometimes simply holding a prop related to the story, such as a stuffed animal, can inspire young readers to recall details from the story. We might prompt young readers to tell about the character or the problem, or have them roll dice to indicate what they should tell about. The retelling map and retelling dice are two tools we can use to guide students in including all the story elements in their retelling.

Retelling Map

The retelling map on page 68 is based on the shape-go map developed by Vicki Benson and Carrice Cummins (2004). It is an excellent tool for teaching students to retell a story. Ideally, you will enlarge the graphic to chart-paper size so students can trace around the shapes with a finger as they retell the beginning, middle, and end of the story. You might even color code the three shapes to match the traffic light colors: green for *go*, yellow for *keep on going*, and red for *stop*. Each shape can also represent elements of the story structure: for example, as you trace around the three sides of the triangle, describe the characters, setting, and problem; trace around the rectangle as you retell the key events in the

Learning Goal: Students will be able to engage in comprehension self-talk as they read.

You can teach students to use gestures to solidify their thinking about their comprehension strategies:
"I wonder…" = a shrug
"I think…" = tap the head
"This reminds me of…" = join fingers to form a chain

Learning Goal: Students will be able to retell key events in the reading, in sequence, using key vocabulary from the text.

story (there may be more than four); finally, the last shape circles back to the beginning to solve the problem and wrap up the story.

Retelling Dice

Create six-sided dice and use sticky labels to place retelling prompts on each side. (On Appendix page 159, you will find instructions for making dice from empty milk cartons.) In both small-group and independent learning, students roll a die and retell the aspect of the story indicated by the prompt:

- *Tell something about one of the characters*
- *Tell something about the setting*
- *Tell something important that happened* (on two sides of the die)
- *Tell about your favorite part*
- *Tell something about the ending*

If students roll a prompt that has already been read, they should add another detail or elaborate on what has been said.

Must-Do

Have students complete the Storybook House graphic organizer on page 69. Demonstrate how to write or draw the characters, setting, and problem in the windows, the solution in the door, and their favorite part in the attic. You can cut out the door and windows, using the dotted lines as folds. Students can draw on one side of each shape and write on the other.

Letter Knowledge and Word-Solving Strategies

At the early stage of reading development, much of the reader's attention is focused on word-level comprehension. Readers at this stage are building their repertoire of automatically recognized words, but they need to devote a lot of energy to negotiating print—making letter–sound connections, identifying letter combinations, and using cueing strategies. This is the time when readers solidify segmenting phonemes to sound out words, then confirming or revisiting those sounds to ensure that reading makes sense.

Most early readers start decoding by focusing on the beginning sounds of words, and sometimes the ending sounds. Now we want them to learn to read right across the word, using the medial vowel sounds as well as the initial and final consonants. We also want them to start recognizing and using consonant combinations, such as blends and digraphs. Teaching routines at this stage should give readers plenty of practice with segmenting (stretching out a word to hear all the sounds) and blending (combining phonemes into a word).

Word Detectives

Learning Goal: Students will be able to identify specific words and letters embedded in connected print.

Word hunts help readers see the relationships between letter concepts and connected print. Just as emergent readers use framers and pointers to find letters in the text (see page 39), early readers hunt for letter patterns and whole words.

Tell students that they are going to be reading detectives and hunt for words that have a particular focus letter, sound, or structure (e.g., plurals, long *a* words, words that have *th*, etc.). Provide each student with a toy magnifying glass and have them hunt through the text to find words that meet the given criteria.

Young readers never seem to tire of the dramatic announcement that "Today's word hunt is sponsored by the long *a*!" You can make it a game by using a random process to select the letter feature, such as drawing a consonant-blend card from a hat or creating a spinner of vowel sounds (see Appendix page 163 for a spinner template).

You can also play I Spy with My Little Eye, with students, having them take turns giving clues to words in the guided-reading text for others to find. Clues might include the initial consonant, a vowel sound, a word within a word, a rhyming word, an inflectional ending (such as -ed), and the like. The other students use a pointer or framer to isolate the word in the text before responding.

Must-Do

Provide each student with a clipboard and pencil and send them on a "write around the room" word hunt. Using the word-level learning focus from the guided reading lesson, have students record words around the room that meet those criteria. At the next guided reading lesson, revisit the students' word lists for sorting, generating sentences, or simply reading aloud.

Flip the Vowel

Learning Goal: Students will be able to use vowel manipulation as a word-solving strategy.

Using a sentence from the current guided-reading text, model for students how you might make a miscue by reading the wrong vowel in a word. For example, if the text says, "Mother and Father Bird made a nest," you might read, "nist." Point out to students that, even though this word looks pretty close and almost sounds right (the beginning and ending sounds are right), it just doesn't make sense in the sentence. The strategy needed to "fix up the mix-up" is to flip the vowel.

As students progress from emergent to early reading, decoding medial vowels is the hardest part of all—especially tricky short-vowel sounds. Start by reviewing the five vowels. Some teachers like to color the vowels on letter tiles to distinguish them from the consonants. Using words taken from the guided-reading text, have students form each focus word with letter tiles.

Tell students that they are going to practice flipping the middle vowel (or boxcar sound, as described on page 38). Using the example of nest, show them how to flip the i to an o. Ask, "Is nost a word? Try flipping the o to an e. Is nest a real word? Does it make sense in our sentence?" Have students practice the routine with other short words from the guided reading text. Each time, they should ask themselves: Is this a real word or not? If the word is embedded in connected text, they ask: Does this word make sense?

If students are comfortable with short-vowel words, you can extent the experience with long vowels with silent -e. Remind students that when we add -e to the end of the word, it doesn't make a sound; however, it does make the middle vowel say its name, so it hitchhikes it on the end of the train after the caboose. For example, if we add an -e to tap, it makes the vowel say long a, so the word is now tape.

Must-Do

Provide students with a list of words to practice flipping the vowel. Instruct them to form each word with letter tiles, then flip flip the vowels to make new words. They write the words they form on a Real Words/Not Real Words sorting mat like the one at the top of the next page.

Real Words	Not Real Words

Karate Chop the Word!

Learning Goal: Students will be able to use root words and inflectional endings to help solve words in reading.

Words with inflectional endings -ed, -ing, and -s account for 90% of all words with suffixes in written English. Send students into the text on a word hunt for words with these endings. They will practice chopping off the endings to look for the root or base words. Start by forming words from the guided-reading text, such as *walking*, with plastic letters or letter tiles. Then chop off the ending, using a "karate chop" action, to separate the root word. At first, you will want to stick to words that have intact roots. If you feel your students are ready, you can include words in which the final consonant is doubled or the final *e* is dropped.

Have students hunt for words from their guided-reading text that have the -ed, -ing, or -s ending. (You might choose to work with only one ending at a time.) Provide each student with five pieces of highlighting tape to highlight these words in their text. Use these words to practice chopping off the endings to look for the familiar root.

Must-Do

Have students take a clipboard and "write around the room," recording words ending in -s, -ed, -ing. They can keep track of their words and see which ending "wins," or has the most words. Sometimes making it a contest engages children who might otherwise be reluctant readers. During the next day's guided reading lesson, use the students' lists to practice chopping words into roots and endings.

Word-Building

Learning Goal: Students will be able to construct words from letter patterns.

Have students use magnetic letters or letter tiles to build words. Manipulating letters helps students engage in active learning as they establish relationships among letter patterns—*top* to *pop* to *mop*, or *tap* to *tape*. Word-building can also be used to reinforce high-frequency words or letter combinations.

The "making words" approach developed by Patricia Cunningham and her colleagues 1992) guides students to build increasingly larger words from patterns, with the teacher instructing the students each step of the way and providing the letters to use. Each student is given a set of letters to create the words individually, then each word is spelled for the group so students can compare their letters to the teacher's. At the end, the students build one big word from all the letters in the set.

Published print and Internet resources will provide many pre-made lessons for making words, but lessons can easily be developed around the guided-reading text. Start by choosing a key word from the story. Make a list of all the words that can be built from the letters in that word. Introduce the words in an order that enables students to build patterns. I also like to add an additional question or action to reinforce the word.

Vary the word-building routine with different types of letters:

- letter tiles (from games like Scrabble)
- plastic letters
- foam letters
- cereal letters
- pasta letters
- letter beads

Example of Word-Building

The word selected is **_parrot_** from the story _All Clean_.

Words to build: at, pat, pot, top, tap, tar, art, part, parrot

Provide students with the following plastic letters or letter tiles:

a	o	p	r	r	t

Provide the following teacher instructions:

- Take two letters, _a_ and _t_, and build the word _at_. We are _at_ school right now.
- Let's add a train engine to the _at_ train by putting _p_ at the beginning. What word do you have? Gently _pat_ your knee with your hand.
- Now let's flip the vowel! Trade the _a_ for _o_, and what do you have? Tell your partner what you can use a _pot_ for.
- Can you flip the letters in _pot_ to make _top_? Put your hands on top of your head.
- Now flip the vowel in _top_ to make _tap_. Tell your partner what you did to change _top_ into _tap_.
- Trade a caboose letter to turn _tap_ into _tar_. Tar is black sticky stuff that is used to fix cracks in roads. What letter did you use?
- Scramble those letters! Use those three letters to make the word _art_.
- I didn't eat the whole chocolate bar, I just ate _part_ of it. What can you add to the front of _art_ to make _part_?
- Now it's time for…Mix and Fix! Take all your letters and scramble them up. Build a word that is a kind of bird from our story.

Extension: Now you know how to make _parrot_. How do you think you could make _carrot_?

An important component of Cunningham's Making Words is sorting all the word cards at the end and using them to make analogies to new words. Because this activity is only one part of the guided reading lesson, you might choose to do these follow-up steps in a subsequent lesson.

Must-Do

Provide each student with 6–8 letter tiles that form a big word from their guided-reading text. Students are to use these tiles to make as many words as they can. They record their words on the Real Word/Not Real Word chart found on page 56.

Word Family Fun

Learning Goal: Students will be able to apply rimes and onsets to solving words in reading.

At the emergent stage, readers learned to identify and generate rhymes. Early readers extend this knowledge by reading and writing rimes—the vowel (or vowel combination) and all the letters that follow it in a syllable, such as _ack_, _est_, _ill_, or _ug_. The wonderful thing about rimes is that, unlike many letter concepts in English, they are reliably phonetic! Vowels in isolation can be counted on to be consistent only about 50% of the time. Consider, for example, the variant _a_ sounds in _ball_, _bar_, _bat_, _bang_, and _bale_. But in rimes, the vowels are consistent more than 75% of the time: e.g., _ball_, _call_, _fall_, _stall_, and so on.

The other advantage of rimes is that they are building blocks for reading and writing many other words. In fact, only 36 basic rimes can be used to form more than 500 basic one-syllable words and countless multi-syllabic words.

Usually, word families are introduced during whole-class instruction, but small-group time is an excellent opportunity to reinforce and practice these very important letter chunks. There will always be opportunities to link words in the guided-reading text to rimes already on the anchor chart. Here are some additional activities for practice with word families during small-group time:

Build Word Ladders

Choose a word from the guided-reading text that contains a rime already on the chunk chart posted in the classroom. With the students, build a ladder of words containing that rime. (This can be done on paper, on the interactive whiteboard, on a whiteboard with masking tape, or in a pocket chart.) With one word for each rung of the ladder, see how high they can climb. (If you assign points to each rung of the ladder, children get practice counting by 2s, 5s, or 10s as they count their points.)

Write Silly Rhymes

Collaboratively compose silly rhymes using at least two words in a word family, using a shared- or interactive-writing approach to record and read them together.

Must-Do

Here are some alternatives for independent practice with rimes and onsets:

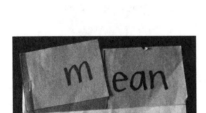

- The Word Family Board Game: Enlarge and reproduce the game board on page 163 so it fits into a file folder. Insert a metal brad into the spinner. Staple a zip-bag to the game board with two playing pieces and a die. Write a familiar rime on each square of the board and an onset letter on each section of the spinner. Students play in partners by taking turns rolling the die and moving their players the appropriate number of spaces on the board. Then they roll the spinner of onsets. If they can make a real word from their rime and onset, they stay where they are. If they can't make a real word, they must move their player back to where it was at the beginning of the turn.
- Word Family Flip Books: Create flip books, as shown at left, with strips of paper about 7.5 cm (3") wide. Cut one 20 cm (8") strip and four 10 cm (4") strips. Stack them and staple along the left side. Have students choose a rime and print it on the strip that sticks out, then write a different onset on each of the shorter strips. They might draw pictures to represent the words, or write a silly rhyme using at least two of the words on the back of the long strip.
- Word Family Card Game: Make two sets of cards: one set of rime cards and one set of onset cards. (Choose from the onset and rime cards provided on page 70.) Label two small gift bags and place each set of cards in its own bag. Have students take turns drawing a card from each bag. If they can form a word from the rime and onset cards, they get to keep the cards; if not, the cards go back into the bags. When all the cards are done, the player with the most cards wins.

High-Frequency Words

One hundred words make up almost half of all the words we read and write. No wonder we call them "high-frequency"! Whether we call them *sight words, popcorn words* (because they keep popping up all over), or *snap words* (because we need to be able to read them in a snap), it's important that these words be recognized automatically. The problem is that many of these words cannot be decoded. Try sounding out *what, of,* or *said*! That's why we use many cues—visual, auditory, and kinesthetic—to embed these words in our minds. We look at the shape of the word, say the individual letters, and clap, sing, or do another action to reinforce the reading and writing of each word.

Common practice in classrooms is to teach three to five words a week in whole-class instruction and post them on a high-frequency–word wall. Once they're on the wall, these are *no-excuse words*. We expect students to be able to read them automatically and write them with ease.

Small-group guided-reading time is an opportunity for students to read and review these words embedded in connected text. During small-group instruction, review the words before reading, hunt for them in the text, and practice writing them after reading. Teaching routines for writing high-frequency words are found in the Reading–Writing Connection on page 65.

Shower Curtain Games

Inexpensive shower curtain liners offer potential for any number of active games for letter and word play. Rule the shower curtain into large squares with a high-frequency word written on each square. Students can walk, hop, or skip along the squares, reading the words as they step on them, or do a beanbag toss and read the word the beanbag lands on. Students like to play "musical words," in which they march on the squares to music with a clipboard in their hands. When the music stops, they read or write the word they are standing on. It's possible to create a variation of Twister in which players are instructed to put their left foot or their right hand on a given word.

Must-Do

- Read it, Make It, Write It: In the learning centre activity pictured here, students read each word in the first column, build it with magnetic letters, then write it on the whiteboard. An alternative is to use a stamp pad to stamp the letters on paper.
- Sight Word Tally: Give each student a marker and a page from a magazine. Given two sight words, they highlight each time they find the words on the page and keep a tally of which word wins (i.e., appears more frequently on the page). It doesn't matter if the students can't read the whole text; the point of the exercise is to practice automatic word recognition. You can use a chart like this:

Word	Number of Times Found

Reading Shortcut Words

Learning Goal: Students will be able to read and construct contractions.

Provide students with the necessary background information:

Sometimes when I'm walking to the mall, I'll take a shortcut across the playground to make my trip a little quicker. We often take shortcuts when we're walking, but we also take shortcuts with words. Instead of saying "I cannot find my keys," I'll take a shortcut and say, "I can't find my keys." Instead of saying, "I will not eat that broccoli," I'll take a shortcut and say, "I won't eat that broccoli." Shortcut words are made by putting two words, like I *and* will, *together and taking out some sounds to make one word—I'll.*

Have students hunt in their guided-reading texts for shortcut words with apostrophes. Use letter tiles to demonstrate how letters are removed and replaced with apostrophes to form contractions. Provide students with their own set of letter tiles and a set of apostrophe tiles to form word pairs such as *I will, he is, they are,* and to remove letters to form contractions.

Must-Do

Use the Read it, Make it, Write it routine from page 59 to have students practice building contractions. Provide students with a set of word cards, each containing two words that can be combined into a contraction (e.g., *can not, have not, she is, I will*). Students read each word pair and construct it with letter tiles, then remove letters and add apostrophes to make the contractions. Provide a strip of paper for them to write the contractions they have formed.

Increasing Fluency

Now that we've painstakingly taught the students how to track every word, it's time to wean them off tracking and word-by-word reading, and instead to encourage reading in phrases. Good early-level text will have line breaks at meaningful phrases to encourage phrase-by-phrase reading.

Sliders for Phrasing

Learning Goal: Students will be able to read in phrases rather than word by word.

Using a passage from the guided-reading text, read aloud, exaggerating the difference between reading word by word and reading in phrases. Invite them to talk about why the latter sounds better and makes more sense. Create a sentence strip excerpted from the guided-reading text and cut it into phrases. Together, read each phrase, saying the words smoothly together.

Point out to students that each line in their guided-reading text is a group of words that go together. Have them finger frame each line and practice reading it smoothly together in chorus several times. Give each student a slider (plastic ruler) to slide under each line as they read, to guide them in reading groups of words smoothly instead of separately.

Must-Do

Have students reread the guided-reading texts in their book boxes with their buddies, using their individual sliders to read in phrases.

Talk Like the Talker

Learning Goal: Students will be able to read dialogue with expression.

Early-level narrative text often introduces dialogue between two characters. Ask students if they can find a place in the text where characters are talking. Talk about how authors indicate to readers when someone is talking, using quotation marks and tag lines such as "she said." Discuss how the voices of different characters might sound different and how clues like *exclaimed* or *whispered* tell us how the character's voice sounds. Have students take turns reading different lines to sound like the character speaking.

Must-Do

Have students reread the text with a buddy, taking turns reading and striving to read dialogue to "talk like the talker." Have them continue this process with other guided-reading texts in their book boxes.

Responding to Reading

Big-Idea Questions

Learning Goal: Students will be able to extend their thinking about a text by participating in guided discussion.

We sometimes assume that early readers—and the texts they read—just don't lend themselves to higher-level thinking. But using appropriate prompting, we can teach our youngest readers to go beyond a totally literal interpretation of the text to examine an author's theme, connections to real life, or deeper inference. Develop a big-idea question for each text that students can discuss with a partner and/or the whole group. Some ideas for big-idea prompts:

- Analyzing the action of characters: *What would you have done?*
- Considering alternative endings: *What might have happened if…?*
- Relating to the theme of the story: *What lesson does this story teach us?*
- Reading critically: *Could this story really happen? Why or why not?*

Must-Do

No must-do is included with this routine, as it focuses on teacher-guided discussion.

Add Some Talking

Learning Goal: Students will be able to anticipate thoughts and comments of characters in a text.

Early-level text often contains dialogue among two or more characters. Show students how to add some talking by using sticky-note speech bubbles. Choose an illustration on any page of the guided-reading text and talk about what the characters might be saying. Add a sticky note to the page and give the characters some dialogue. Point out to students that text usually includes a tag line (e.g., "he said") but it's not necessary when they use speech bubbles.

Must-Do

Provide students with three or four sticky notes (if possible, find sticky notes in the shape of speech bubbles) to insert into the text, either at their discretion or your direction, and use them to write possible dialogue.

Book Review

Learning Goal: Students will be able to evaluate a text that they have read.

Offering opinions or evaluations of what has been read should not be difficult for young readers. Explaining why they feel the way they do about a text might be more challenging. Ask children to explain with questions such as these:

- *What part of the story did you like best? Why did you like it?*
- *If you were the writer, what might you change? Why would you change that?*
- *Would you like the character for a friend? Why or why not?*

Must-Do

The Book Review form on page 71 is a starting point for written response and provides an overview of a student's understanding of the story. It integrates a summary with describing a favorite part and identifying new vocabulary.

The Reading–Writing Connection

Interactive writing is a powerful structure to help children learn the processes of putting thoughts down on paper. During an interactive writing lesson, students and teacher compose a text together and the students take turns "sharing the pen" to write the ideas on paper with teacher support. (See sample below.) Small-group reading is an excellent opportunity to give students the chance to share the pen as they generate responses to reading. Some guidelines for interactive writing:

- Divide the paper in half: a practice space at the top and space for the actual writing at the bottom. Use the practice space for teaching.
- Use "book writing" rather than invented spelling.
- Compose ideas together and have students take turns writing the words.
- Assign one student to be the "spacer," whose job it is to place his/her hand after each word to create a space.
- Reread the text together after every few words to make sure it's making sense.
- Be prepared for a text to take more than one period to write. This is a slow process.
- Find ways to keep the students on the floor engaged: e.g., tracing words on the rug; spying around the room for words; or writing words on their individual whiteboards.

At no stage of literacy development is the reading–writing connection as symbiotic as during the early reading–writing stage. Like early readers, early writers have an increasing repertoire of high-frequency words and are beginning to apply letter–sound correspondences to the words they write. Writing may be an even more effective tool for phonics instruction than reading, because it calls for active learning.

Readers at this stage	Writers at this stage
• use letters, words, and pictures to get information from books • have mastered most concepts about print, including directionality and distinguishing pictures from print • begin to understand spaces around words • connect letters and sounds to decode during reading • add some high-frequency words automatically • begin to understand sentences as groups of words with punctuation • prefer to read topics relating to their personal experience • move beyond patterned text • can cope with more than one line on a page • can retell what was read	• use letters, words, and pictures to tell stories and convey ideas • begin to write in lines from left to right, top to bottom • begin to understand spaces around words • connect letters and sounds to spell during writing • write some high-frequency words conventionally • begin to write sentences with capitals and punctuation • prefer to write about topics relating to their personal experience • coordinate pictures and writing on the page • can relate more than one detail in writing • will try to write most words in speaking vocabulary

Bubblegum Writing

When early writers begin to use the phonetic principle for writing, most start by using only consonants, often using one letter to represent an entire word. Gradually, initial and final consonants appear, followed by medial vowels. Ultimately, our goal for early readers is that they use a letter to represent every sound they hear, a practice known as invented, phonetic, or temporary spelling—or what I call *bubblegum writing*:

> Pretend the word is a piece of bubblegum in your mouth. Pretend to stretch the word out with one hand, slowly saying the sounds, while using the other hand to write a letter for every sound that you hear.

For early writers, there are two ways to spell a word—bubblegum writing or book writing. In bubblegum writing, we stretch out the word like a piece of bubblegum from our mouth and write a letter for every sound we hear.

The phonemic awareness work emergent readers engaged in as they stretched out the sounds of words and snapped them back together now extends to alphabet letters and the phonetic principle. Invented spelling requires the integration of phonemic awareness and phonics, as they stretch out a word and represent every sound that they hear with a letter. Small-group reading time provides an ideal opportunity to engage in active and interactive letter–sound practice with teacher support.

Using words from the guided-reading text, start with phonetically regular CVC (consonant–vowel–consonant) words, then gradually move on to more challenging words. Remind students that, while book writing looks the same for everyone, bubblegum writing can differ from one writer to another.

At this stage, children have a limited reading vocabulary, but they can write any word they can say. There is extensive evidence that phonetic spelling helps students become spelling problem-solvers and helps them construct deeper understandings about how our language goes together. This is why it's important to empower them with the ability to spell phonetically and to encourage them to add more details.

Beginning/Middle/End Books

One of the biggest challenges in working with early writers is to get them beyond one detail. Stapling three pages together to make a book and inviting students to draw and write about three things that happened in the story helps guide them toward increasing detail. Practice retelling the beginning, middle, and end of the story by tapping on the front, middle, and back page of the book as you tell. Have students illustrate and add captions to the three parts of the story in their books.

Text Innovations

Using patterns and springboards from their reading can help many young readers build the confidence they need to be independent writers and can get them over the hurdle of "one detail, now I'm done." Be judicious about the use of patterned writing; we don't want students to become dependent on frameworks. But sometimes texts like *The Important Book* by Margaret Wise Brown (use template below) or *How to Be* by Lisa Brown (see sample below) can teach creative structures for writing about reading.

Important Thing

The important thing about _____ is

_____.

It/they _____.

It/they _____.

And it/they _____.

But the important thing about _____ is

_____.

How to be a Valentine

By Hailey

Lay in the envelope,
Get written on,
Let People open you.

Spelling High-Frequency Words

It's important that students are able to automatically write, as well as read, common high-frequency words. Here are some small-group instruction activities to support practice writing high-frequency words:

Read My Mind

This success-oriented game, developed by Patricia Cunningham (1998), provides important practice in locating and writing words from the high-frequency word wall. Choose a word from the word wall that is also found in the current guided-reading text. Invite students to "read your mind" to guess the word you have chosen. Have students write the numbers 1 to 5 on their paper or whiteboard. You will provide five clues and, for each clue, they must guess the word. They can write the same word more than once, but they must write a word each time. Start with a vague clue: "It's a word on the word wall." With each subsequent clue, get a little more specific: "It has one syllable; the vowel is *a*; it starts with *f*; it rhymes with *ball*." By the fifth clue, students should have guessed the word correctly.

X-Ray Eyes

Margo Southall (2009) uses this activity to help students visualize and internalize sight words. Remove letters, one at a time, from a known word, and teach students to "see and say" the missing letters. Write a word and chant the letters with the students. As you erase one letter at a time, invite the children to put on their x-ray eyes (form circles around their eyes with their thumbs and forefingers) to visualize the whole word and spell all the missing letters in sequence, until the entire word has been erased. Repeat the game, with students selecting and erasing letters in the word.

Sample Guided Reading Lesson Plan for Early Readers

Group: mid-early level

Title	Learning Goals
Baby Canada Goose Flies South	Comprehension: Self-monitoring, retelling Word Study: HF Words, Contractions Fluency: Reading phrases

Text/Book Introduction

Preview:

Invite students to identify the pictures on the cover. Tell them the name of the book: Baby Canada Goose Flies South. *This is a book about a family of geese and it is the baby's first time to fly south for the winter.* Point out the page numbers at the bottom of each page. *What do you think Baby Goose's problem will be? How do you think the story will end? Take your own picture walk and talk to your reading partner bout what you see in the pictures. Make sure to look for the details in the pictures.*

Prior Knowledge:

Turn and talk with a partner about why the geese fly south. How do you think the baby goose feels on her first flight? On the cover, which goose do you think is the baby? Why? Where do you think they are? What season is it? How do you know?
HF Word Review: *one, now, will, come, want, here* Write each word on a sentence strip. Place the sentence strips in a large envelope and reveal the word, one letter at a time, for children to guess.
New Words: Use letter tiles for word building—*south*; little word *out*; apply to *shout*.

Purpose:

Read the story to see how Baby Goose learns to fly south. As you read, please talk to your brain about the three questions we've talked about. Reinforce the three questions of self-monitoring: Does my reading make sense? Does it sound right? Does it look right? *If the answer to any of those questions is "no" then I need to go back and try to fix up my reading.*
Remember to read in a whisper voice, and if you finish, go back and read it again. See how many times you can read the book before I tell you to stop.

Day 1	Must-Do
• Provide book introduction, distribute books, and stagger start the reading. • As children read, provide ongoing listening and support for decoding and comprehension. Ensure that each student has read through the book at least twice. • After reading: Celebrate strategy use and review three keys to self-monitoring. Read a few sentences to students with deliberate errors. *How do you know this is wrong? "I don't went to fly south."'* • Retelling Map: Have students take turns tracing the shapes on the retelling map as they retell. 1. Beginning: Who was the story about? Where and when did it take place? What was the problem? 2. Middle: What happened first, next, last? 3. End: How was the problem solved?	Complete a graphic organizer book review of the story.

Day 2	Must-Do
• Provide opportunity to reread text independently. • Look Who's Talking: Talk about how the characters in the story might say their words. Look for clues like exclamation ("excited" marks) and dialogue tags (*cried, shouted*). Page 5: *"I don't want to fly south!" cried Baby Goose.* Page 9: *"I can't fly very far," he cried.* Page 10: *"Let's go!" shouted Father Goose.* Invite students to take turns reading using appropriate expression. • Word Study: Shortcut Words *it's, don't, let's* Use letter tiles to form *it is*. Take out the second *i* and replace it with an apostrophe. • Big-idea Question: *We've been talking about how it helps us understand our reading when we connect it to something we've done or learned about or seen or read in another book. Baby Canada Goose was afraid to try something new, but he kept trying and got some help and was able to solve his problem. Talk to your partner about a connection you make to this story.*	• More shortcut word practice with sentence strips or letter tiles: *isn't, can't, he's.* Have students write and illustrate sentences about the story using their shortcut words. • Buddy read the text with appropriate expression.

Sketch and Label

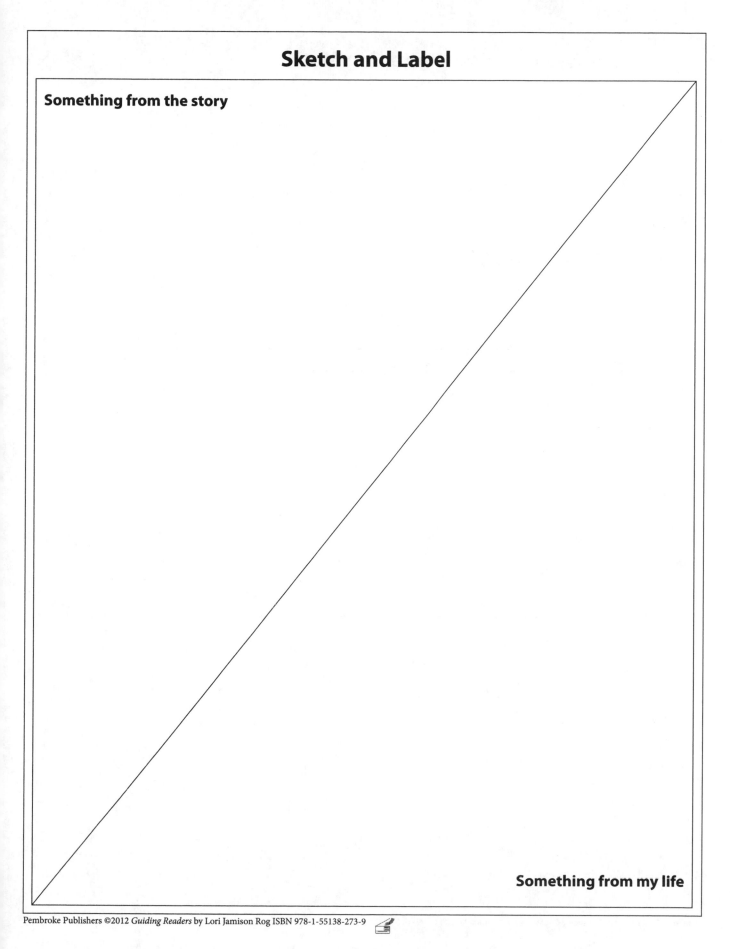

Something from the story

Something from my life

Pembroke Publishers ©2012 *Guiding Readers* by Lori Jamison Rog ISBN 978-1-55138-273-9

Retelling Map

Green

Yellow

Red

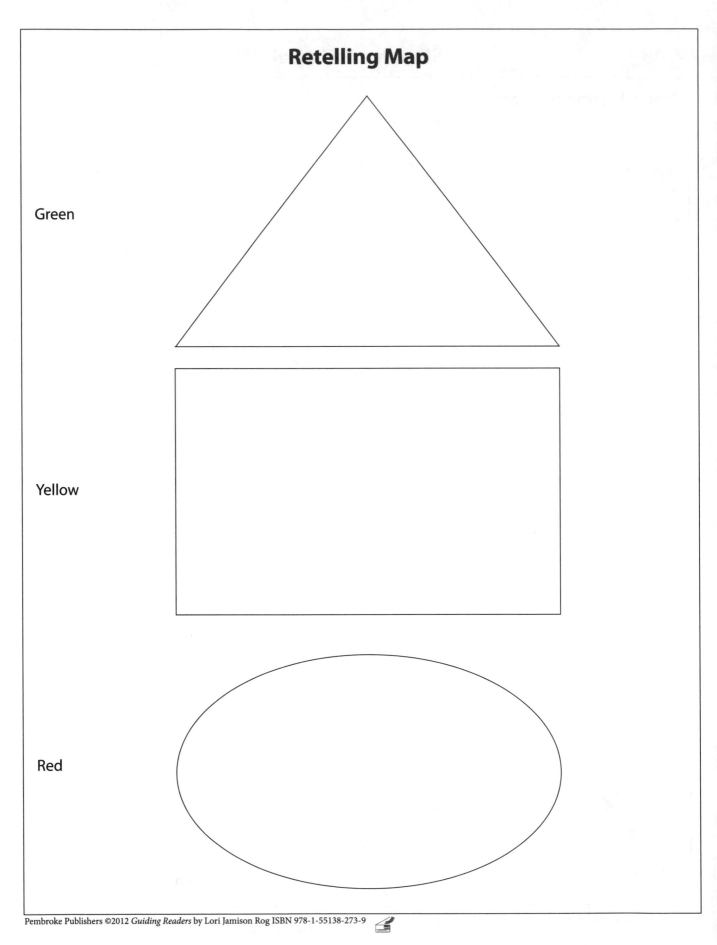

Pembroke Publishers ©2012 *Guiding Readers* by Lori Jamison Rog ISBN 978-1-55138-273-9

Storybook House

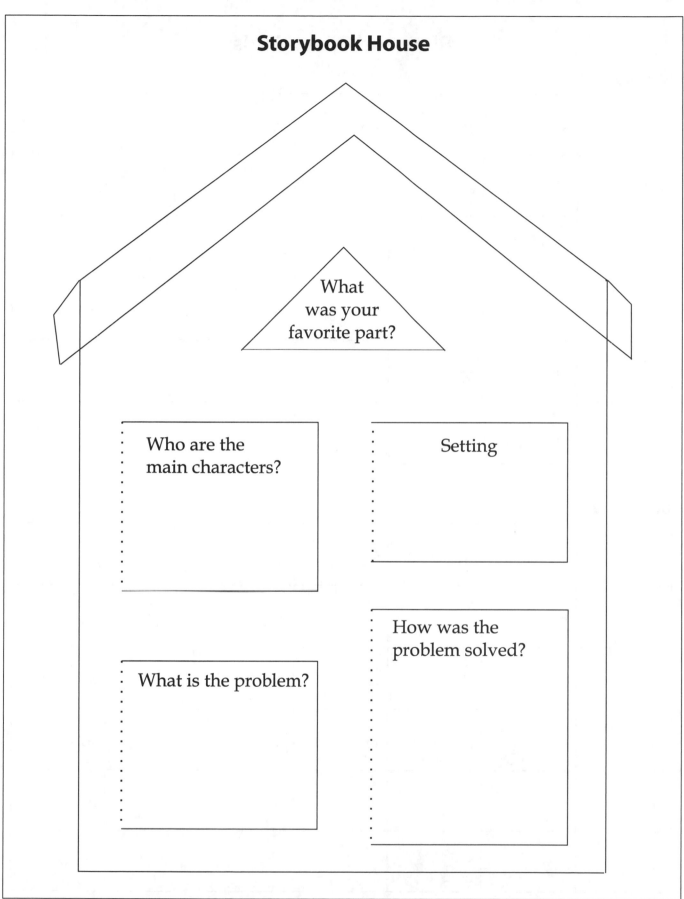

What
was your
favorite part?

Who are the
main characters?

Setting

What is the problem?

How was the
problem solved?

Pembroke Publishers ©2012 *Guiding Readers* by Lori Jamison Rog ISBN 978-1-55138-273-9

Rime and Onset Cards

Rime Cards

ack	ain	ake	ale	all	ame	an
ank	ap	ash	at	ate	aw	ay
eat	ell	est	ice	ick	ide	ight
ill	in	ing	ink	ip	it	ock
oke	old	op	ore	ot	uck	ug
ump	unk					

Onset Cards

b	c	d	f	g	h	l
m	n	p	r	s	t	w
bl	br	cl	cr	dr	fl	fr
gl	br	pl	pr	sl	sp	spl
st	str	tr	wr	ch	sh	th
wh						

Pembroke Publishers ©2012 *Guiding Readers* by Lori Jamison Rog ISBN 978-1-55138-273-9

Book Review

by _____

The title of this story is _____

It was about _____

_____ .

Some important words from this book

A picture of my favorite part

5

Guiding Developing Readers

Rachel is a fan of the Magic Treehouse books. Even though some of the books are a little hard for her, Rachel has enough background knowledge about the characters and the text structure to understand and enjoy them, and she has read several books in the series. She likes the idea that her book has many chapters; it makes her feel grown-up in her reading. Rachel's favorite routine at school is buddy reading. She and her reading buddy particularly enjoy the titles in the series that are about dinosaurs. Rachel says that these books are "like reading facts and a story at the same time."

Rachel and her reading buddy are in Grade 2 and are considered to be *developing readers*. This is often described as a transitional stage between oral and silent reading, between tracking and fluency, and between word-level and text-level comprehension.

Developing readers have a large repertoire of words they recognize automatically and a range of strategies for figuring out unfamiliar words. Because they don't need to devote as much energy to reading individual words, they can pay more attention to higher-level text comprehension. This is a time to reinforce comprehension strategies, such as predicting, inferring, and generating mental images.

These readers have more capacity for holding several details in their heads and enjoy reading chapter books and longer nonfiction texts. Developing readers are beginning to recognize the difference between fiction and nonfiction, and know how to use informational texts to locate specific information. Readers at this stage can appreciate and distinguish make-believe characters and situations from "real" ones, so imaginative texts such as folktales, science fiction, and fantasy begin to gain popularity.

As well, readers at this stage

- have a large repertoire of sight words and a wide range of strategies for word-solving
- enjoy longer texts, such as chapter books
- are learning to read silently, listening to the voice in their heads
- demonstrate increasing fluency, phrasing, and expression when they read orally
- can draw on different sources of background knowledge, such as personal experience, other books, movies, or world events
- can draw basic inferences as they read

- generally self-monitor and know when they don't understand what they are reading
- don't need illustrations, but often enjoy them
- ask and answer questions about their reading
- can support ideas and opinions with evidence from the text
- understand the basic foundations of story structure: characters, setting, problem, solution
- can distinguish imaginative from realistic characters and situations
- use informational texts to answer a question or find out facts
- are beginning to recognize different genres and text forms

Students at this stage are making the transition from oral to silent reading, so we want to remind them to listen to their voices in their heads. For students needing more practice in oral-reading fluency, we continue to have them read aloud during guided reading, just as in the emergent and early stages. However, at some point we want them to read silently, and it's always a good idea to give them the opportunity to read texts silently to themselves before reading them aloud to the group. We can still shoulder-tap students to raise their voices for a few seconds while we listen to them, but no student should have to publicly read aloud a text he/she has never read before.

As students read, they can be tracking their thinking by using sticky notes to tab key ideas, vocabulary, strategy spots, or other points in the text. The Reading Toolkit (see page 28) is a convenient organizer for a variety of sticky notes to use during the guided reading lesson.

Texts for Developing Readers

There is a much greater range of topics and text structures in developing-level text than in previous stages. Readers at this stage are no longer limited to reading about ideas that are within their range of personal experience. Most readers are able to distinguish between make-believe and reality in books and start to enjoy imaginative stories like folktales, fantasy, and fables. Their range of nonfiction reading also expands, as they learn to read for specific information or for answers to questions.

Like our friend Rachel, many developing readers get hooked on series books. There are several aspects of series books that support developing readers: predictable plot structures, consistent levels of difficulty, common characters and themes. Developing-level text has some vocabulary control, but there are fewer repeated words and more unique vocabulary and concepts. Students are expected to be able to go beyond sounding out to use a range of word-solving strategies.

In spite of increased volume of print and length of story, most developing-level text remains fairly simplistic. Because the majority of sentences are either simple or compound (i.e., two independent clauses joined by a conjunction such as *and*, *but*, *or*, or *because)*, the text often sounds choppy to the ear.

Other characteristics of developing level text:

- few or no illustrations
- print and illustrations integrated on the page in different ways
- separate chapters, with or without headings
- text in block paragraphs
- increasing amounts of unique vocabulary

The website www.kidsreads.com lists, among other books, series for all ages and interests. Some popular series for developing readers:
- Arthur by Marc Brown
- Junie B. Jones by Barbara Park
- Magic Treehouse by Mary Pope Osborne
- Henry and Mudge by Cynthia Rylant
- Nate the Great by Marjorie Sharmat
- Star Wars Step into Reading by various authors
- Commander Toad by Jane Yolen

- varied fonts and unique text features
- several characters, episodic plots
- 16 pages or more in length; may have several chapters
- wide range of topics and themes beyond the reader's personal experience

Although readers at this stage are keen to read chapter books and beginning novels, we need to be cautious about using these texts for guided reading. As mentioned earlier in the book, longer texts can vary considerably in reading difficulty from one chapter to the next. Publishers will sometimes provide a readability or grade-level score, but such a calculation based on an average of the whole book does not necessarily reflect the page-by-page challenges in the book. Even if a text is consistently leveled, it simply takes too long to read a whole book in guided reading lessons. Certainly it's appropriate, however, to read a chapter or other excerpt from a chapter book (as in the sample lesson on page 87). In fact, sometimes guiding students through one chapter of the book will provide just enough support to enable them to read the rest of the book on their own.

What a Story! by Paul Kropp, illustrated by Loris Lesynski (Scholastic, 2003). Reprinted with permission of Paul Kropp and Loris Lesynski.

"Yes. They said I was very brave. They might even give me a medal."

Sara smiled. Ms. Tuddle clapped her hands. Everyone forgot about her story.

10

Chapter 4

The next month, the class studied weather. Ms. Tuddle said, "I want all of you to imagine what it's like to be in a big storm. Then write a story about it."

11

The Guided Reading Lesson for Developing Readers

As with other stages, the guided reading lesson for developing readers consists of a book introduction, scaffolded independent reading of a carefully selected text, and revisiting the text for different purposes.

After the book introduction, students read short segments of the text independently. We may read only one or two pages at a time, then stop to discuss the content and reading process before moving on to the next section of text. After reading, students generally engage in some form of written response.

See page 87 for a sample guided reading lesson sequence plan for developing readers.

Before Reading

Features of the Guided Reading Lesson for Developing Readers

BEFORE READING
- Text introduction

DURING READING
- Transition from oral to silent reading
- Sticky notes to track thinking and strategies
- Comprehension strategy focus

AFTER READING
- Fluency work
- Focus on vocabulary and text structures
- Written responses

At this stage, the concepts and topics of the guided-reading text might be beyond the direct experience of the readers, so special attention must be paid to activating prior knowledge. We are no longer likely to take a picture walk, but we might draw students' attention to some illustrations (if there are any) or invite students to do their own picture walk to prepare for reading. Our purpose for reading is likely to focus on a comprehension strategy, such as connecting, questioning, inferring, self-monitoring, or synthesizing, or it might be the application of a range of strategies to process the text. Because there may be unique vocabulary, it is worth considering which words, if any, to preteach. Always remember, however, that words are learned more deeply and retained longer when they are introduced in the context of the reading. If an unfamiliar word is essential to understanding the gist of the text, we should preteach it. If there are enough supports for readers to solve the word on their own, we should give them a chance to do so.

During Reading

Groups who struggle with oral reading fluency should continue to read the text aloud in a soft voice, as in the emergent and early stages. This enables them to hear their own reading and attend more to pacing, phrasing, and expression. However, we want developing readers to gradually make the transition to reading silently.

We generally read only a short chunk of text at a time, especially if students are reading silently. I will choose a pause point, usually no more than a page or two, and instruct students to place the sticky-note Stop signs from their Reading Toolkits (see page 28) at the stopping point. Students read to the stopping point (and go back and reread, if they finish before the others), often tracking their thinking during reading or identifying strategy spots with sticky notes, as instructed.

Often we will read to process the print during the first reading, reserving our sticky-note reading for subsequent rereadings. When all students reach the stopping point, we pause to discuss the text and the reading processes used, usually in partners, then with the whole group. Then we reposition our Stop signs at another pause point and continue the routine. We often go back into a section of text previously read to look for information, to find support for an idea, or to read bits aloud.

On the second reading, we refocus our purpose. Maybe we revisit the text to consider comprehension strategies, perhaps to make connections or draw inferences. I find that on the first reading most students are devoting their reading energy to simply making sense of the text on the surface, and if we wait until the second reading to focus metacognitively on strategies, students are more likely to think deeply about the text and their reading process.

Only after the comprehension goal has been addressed do we focus on a word-level goal. Most students at this stage are quite competent at decoding phonetically, so word study might focus on other word-solving strategies, such as context clues or root words and affixes.

If we are using a beginning chapter book or novel, we read an excerpt of only one or two chapters in the guided reading sequence. As mentioned, close reading and rereading are not appropriate for an entire novel, but guided reading of a couple of chapters might provide enough support for readers to complete the rest of the book on their own.

After Reading

Never stop at one question! When prompting or questioning students for higher-level thinking, always ask students to support or extend their thinking after responding.

Texts at the developing stage generally offer more layers of comprehension than at earlier levels, and we often spend a lot of time discussing, interpreting, and evaluating what we have read. Students at this stage should be encouraged to support their opinions and responses with references to the text. Must-do activities focus on extending experiences with the text, reinforcing text-level or word-level comprehension strategies, or engaging in written responses to reading. These students are capable of crafting a range of different written responses. Graphic organizers help students collect and categorize information about their reading.

Fluent, phrased reading is particularly important at this stage of development because the texts contain longer and more complex sentences. If students are still barking out each word, they lose track of overall meaning. There are many ways we can support fluency practice after reading, ranging from simply rereading familiar texts to performing readers theatre scripts.

Sample Areas of Focus

Purposeful Use of Comprehension Strategies

- Articulating strategy use (metacognition)
- Locating specific information in the text
- Beginning to support inferences during reading
- Consciously creating mental images during reading
- Identifying and using different text features (e.g., charts, labeled diagrams, maps, captions, glossaries, etc.) to locate and retrieve information during reading
- Adjusting and confirming predictions throughout reading
- Analyzing relationship of illustrations with text message
- Identifying transition words that signal sequence in text
- Knowing the difference between information that is directly stated ("in the book") and information that must be inferred ("in my head")

Increasing Range of Word-Solving Strategies and Vocabulary Development

- Purposeful and integrated use of
  - Context clues
  - Chunking words by syllables
  - Phonetic clues: reading into the word to blend all sounds
  - Medial sounds and letter combinations
  - Looking for familiar word parts from known words
  - Common prefixes and inflectional endings (e.g., *ing*, *ed*, *s*)
- Identifying relationships among words, especially homophones (same sound, different spelling and meaning), antonyms, synonyms
- Recognizing and using interesting and descriptive words from reading

Reading Fluently, with Expression, Speed, and Phrasing

- Pausing at punctuation and not at end of lines

- Pacing and expression that convey meaning
- Making the transition from oral to silent reading
- Automatic recognition of grade-appropriate high-frequency words

Responding to Reading

- Identifying key ideas in text
- Identifying characters, setting, problem, solution
- Beginning to critique texts and offer support for opinions
- Analyzing characters from what they say and do and from what is said about them
- Comparing two texts
- Writing in response to a prompt

Lesson Routines

Comprehension Strategies

How Do You Know?

Learning Goal: Students will be able to find information in the text to support ideas and opinions.

One important skill for developing readers is the ability to search a text for specific information or detail. In this routine, students locate answers in the text to specific questions.

Prepare some *how do you know?* questions that are directly answered in the guided-reading text that has already been read. Students should hunt for the answers and highlight them in their texts using strips of removable highlighting tape. (Encouraging students to highlight the information enables you to quickly and easily assess their responses.)

When students demonstrate their ability to locate specific details or find answers in the text to literal questions, extend the experience to more inferential questions. Tell students that sometimes they can't find the answer to *how do you know?* right there in the text. But the author almost always gives clues. For example, in the sample text *What a Story!*, the author doesn't specify that this story takes place in a school, but there are clues. We might ask the students to be reading detectives and look for clues that the story takes place in a school. Develop a set of basic inference questions or prompts, and invite students to look for the clues to the answers.

Must-Do

Provide students with four to six questions from the guided-reading text. Have them use highlighting tape or underline with sticky strips the answers or the clues to the answers. They should number sticky strips that correspond to the numbered questions. During the next guided reading lesson, review students' answers and compare their answers and interpretations.

In the Book or in My Head?

Learning Goal: Students will be able to self-question as they read and determine answers through literal or inferential understanding.

Good readers ask questions when they read. They wonder things all the time: why a character is behaving as he/she is; what will happen next; or why something doesn't seem to make sense. This lesson provides students with practice in asking questions and determining how the answer is found—directly in the text (literal) or inferred from clues in the text and the reader's background knowledge.

Remind students that they have been practicing "I wonders" during read-aloud time. Good readers wonder things all the time. Sometimes, their wonderings are answered right there in the book as they continue reading; sometimes there are clues in the text to guide their thinking but they have to use their own ideas to answer their wonderings.

Have students read a section of text and tab two or three spots where they wondered something. At the end of the reading, record the students' wonderings on a chart like the one below and discuss whether they found answers to their questions as they read. Were the answers found directly in the text? Or were there clues that the reader has to use to think of the answers? Have students look back into the text for answers, or clues to the answers, to the wonderings on the chart. Remind students that *in the book* questions will be answered with "I know" and *in my head questions* will be answered with "I think." Then code the wonderings with a book symbol for "in the book" (literal) answers or a head symbol for "in my head" (inferential) answers.

Wondering	Answering	Coding 📖 in the book 👤 in my head
I wonder...	I think/I know...	
I wonder...	I think/I know....	

Must-Do

- Give students another text at their independent level (or another chapter from the same chapter book, as long as it's at an appropriate level). Have them read and tab three to six wonderings, in preparation for the next guided reading lesson. They should write their wonderings directly on the sticky notes as a record for the next lesson.
- Have students read a section from a text of their choice and tab three to four wonderings. Complete an "I Wonder" flap book (see Appendix page 161 for directions on making a flap book). On each of the top flaps, they write one wondering. Under each flap, they answer the wondering with an "I know..." or an "I think..."

Traffic-Light Transition Words

Words like *first*, *next*, *that night*, or *finally* give the reader clues about the timing, sequence, or order in which events in the story occur. In this lesson, students look for transition words and then use them to retell the story.

Choose a text that has at least five or six transition words or phrases. (Procedural or how-to text is good for this purpose.) After reading, have students go on a hunt for words that give clues to the order in which things happen. Talk about how these kinds of words help us understand what we read.

Create a chart of *green-light words* that indicate beginning (such as *first*), *yellow-light words* that indicate middle (such as *then, also, the next day*), and *red-light words* that indicate ending (such as *finally* or *in the end*).

Learning Goal: Students will be able to use transition words to help them understand sequence of text.

Traffic-Light Words

Green-light words include *first, to begin with, at the start.*
Yellow-light words include *then, later, after a while, meanwhile, suddenly.*
Red-light words include *last, finally, at the end.*

Must-Do

Fold a piece of paper into four sections. Choose one green-light word, two yellow-light words, and one red-light word and write them in the four sections. Retell the story in four parts, each starting with one of the transition words.

Text-to-Text Connections

Learning Goal: Students will be able to use connections to other reading to support comprehension.

Readers must use their background knowledge to make sense of text. That background knowledge sometimes comes from experiences we've had directly, and sometimes it comes from other things that we have read. This lesson reinforces text-to-text comparisons.

Choose an instructional-level text that is connected in some way to a text that has been previously read; for example,

- another variation of a familiar tale
- another book in a series
- another book by the same author
- another book on the same topic or theme

Remind students about the strategy of making text-to-text connections. After reading, talk about ways that the book is similar to or different from another that has been read. Create a comparison chart (see Appendix page 160 for a foldable comparison chart) and, together, record the similarities and unique features of each book.

Must-Do

Provide students with another text at their independent-reading level and have them tab two or three points that remind them of other reading. They should jot their text-to-text connections down on the sticky notes to discuss at the next guided reading lesson.

Click—Take a Picture!

Learning Goal: Students will be able to create mental images from printed text.

This is the first stage at which readers are likely to encounter full pages of text without illustrations. Research tells us that generating mental images during reading contributes significantly to comprehension by helping readers organize, remember, and retrieve information they have read (Gambrell & Koskinen, 2002). For many readers, this process comes naturally; reading a book is like watching a movie running through their minds. For others, however, visualizing must be taught, practiced, and purposefully applied.

Plan pause points during the reading for students to *click* (make a gesture like taking a picture with a camera) and tell a partner about what pictures they have in their minds at that point.

If you have an illustrated text, flip the process and have students add words to the pictures. You may want to show students some samples of captioned pictures (from newspapers or magazines, for example), so they get a sense of how a caption is more than a title, but is a sentence describing what's happening in the picture and how it connects to the story.

Must-Do

- Have students generate visuals to represent aspects of the story. They might create a three-part storyboard to illustrate and label the beginning, middle, and end of the story. (You might adapt the Story Wheel retelling tool described on page 126 in chapter 7.)
- Students can sketch their favorite part of the story, the most exciting part, or the part that inspired the most vivid mental picture for them.
- Another alternative is to have students add sticky-note captions to at least three additional illustrations in the story.

There are three ways that we learn about characters during reading:

- What the author directly states about the character
- What the character says, thinks, or does
- What others say about or how they interact with the character

Fictional texts at the developing level often ask readers to distinguish among several characters. Sometimes information about a character is directly stated by the author or by another character in the book; at other times, readers must make inferences about the character from his or her words or actions. Developing readers need to be able to analyze character traits and how they are conveyed in the text.

Students don't always have a language to talk about character traits, and it's a good idea to build this vocabulary during whole-class instruction. You may even want to create anchor charts of possible words to use to talk about characters, such as the one below.

Character Traits Anchor Chart

Some words to describe characters

hard-working	lazy	fair	unfair
honest	dishonest	brave	cowardly
afraid	fearless	foolish	clever
friendly	rude	kind	cruel
generous	greedy	cheerful	sad
angry	happy	gentle	mean
lonely	friendly	funny	serious
good at…	bad at…	likes…	dislikes…

Choose one of the main characters in the guided-reading story and discuss with students the character traits (personality and appearance) as well as clues to these traits in the text. Have students revisit the text to look for specific evidence or clues. You might record this information on a chart.

Must-Do

- Create a Venn diagram or comparison chart to compare two characters. (Instructions for making a Foldable Comparison Chart are on Appendix page 160.)
- Make a Character Report Card (see template on page 88). As a group, create a list of character traits on which to evaluate the character (known as *subjects* on the report card). Then have students work independently or in pairs to give the character a rating for each trait. The most important aspect of this task is the report card Comments, in which students have to explain the rating.
- Create a Character Chart (you can use the double Four-Square Organizer described in step 5 on Appendix page 159). In the centre shape, write the character's name. In the four shapes around the centre, write four traits or characteristics that describe the character. In the outside corners, write the clues from the text that explain those traits. For example, in the sample lesson from *What a Story!* we might identify one of Sara's characteristics as "imaginative." The evidence from the text is that she makes up incredible stories to explain why she can't write a story.

Word-Solving Strategies

Developing readers have acquired a range of cueing systems to solve unfamiliar words. They know how to look into the word to blend all the sounds. However, many of the challenging words readers encounter at the developing stage are not decodable or are too long to blend all the sounds. Furthermore, readers might be able to say the word, but that doesn't necessarily help them understand it. At this stage, the key emphases are helping students derive meaning from the words they read, building vocabulary, and decoding by letter patterns and chunks.

How to Read a Word You Don't Know

1. Chunk the word into syllables and blend the syllables together. Does it sound right? Does it make sense in the sentence?
2. If not, try another way to say it. Try flipping the vowel sound.
3. Look for word parts that you know.
4. If you're not sure what the word means, try reading around the word for clues to its meaning.
5. If all else fails, look up the word in a dictionary or ask for help.

Reading around the Word

Learning Goal: Students will be able to use context clues to determine the meaning of unfamiliar words.

Often authors, especially in nonfiction, will give clues in the text to help readers solve difficult words. In this lesson students learn to "read around the word" to look for context clues.

Choose an excerpt from an instructional-level text that contains some unfamiliar vocabulary supported by context clues. (Often, informational text is the best choice.) Draw students' attention to one of the challenging words by printing that word on a card and having students locate the word in their texts. Tell students that sometimes authors give us clues to the meaning of tricky words in the other words on the page. We call this "reading around the word." Have students use strips of highlighting tape to highlight other words on the page that help us understand the tricky word. Talk about all the clues that students have identified and, as a group, build a definition of the focus word.

Continue with another tricky word from the text; this time, have students work in pairs to read around the word for clues and construct a definition based on the clues.

Must-Do

Provide students with a section of independent-level (easy-peasy) text or a previous guided-reading text that contains a few unfamiliar vocabulary words that are supported by context clues. Provide a list of three or four words from the text for students to find and define. Have students work in pairs to write each word, record clue words or phrases from the text, and create their own definitions based on the clue words, such as in the graphic organizer on page 88.

More Word Family Fun

Learning Goal: Students will be able to use rimes to solve words.

On page 58, we talked about building a chunk chart of anchor words for rimes and onsets. This process can be continued with developing readers, as we reinforce the basic rimes and add new ones. During small-group guided reading, revisit the chunk chart and reinforce patterns that are encountered in the text.

Invite students to go on a word hunt in their guided-reading text for chunk chart words.

Here are two more active shower-curtain games to add to those described in the previous chapter (page 59). These can be introduced in the small group and played independently as a must-do. Prepare a game board by ruling a shower curtain liner into squares and write a word-family anchor word in each square.

1. Students take turns rolling a die and moving the appropriate number of squares on the game board. Whatever word they land on, they must provide a rhyming word in the same family. Make up your own rules for moving forward or back. (Perhaps a student might have one or two "lifelines" to ask others for help?)

2. Provide each student with his/her own copy of a sheet that matches the grid on the game board. They toss a bean bag onto a square and must 1) read the word; 2) say a rhyming word; 3) write the rhyming word on their own card in the appropriate square. The first person to black out their card or complete a requisite number of squares is the winner.

Must-Do

After the games have been introduced during small-group time, students can play the games in pairs during independent learning.

Chunking Long Words

Many of the words that challenge developing readers have more than one syllable. Teach students not to fear big words, because often big words are easy syllables joined together.

Most classrooms have word-family charts on display, but too often students don't know how to use them as resources for reading and writing. In this lesson, students practice applying familiar chunks to decode unfamiliar words.

Draw students' attention to a multisyllabic word in the text, such as *department* (see sample in margin). Draw "waves" under the syllables. (At this stage, teaching rules for dividing words into syllables is less important than teaching students to look and listen for rimes.) Ask them to look at the chunk chart to see which anchor word might help them decode each syllable.

Encourage students to verbalize their thinking: "This syllable has the same chunk as *cart*, but it starts with *p* so it must be *part*."

Not every syllable will have (or need) an anchor word from the chunk chart. Readers usually have to draw on more than one type of connection to use what they already know about letter patterns. Teach students to look for little words in big words, similarities to familiar words, connections to root words, and letter patterns. For example, when figuring out the word *believer*, they might relate it to words like teacher (someone who teaches) or singer (someone who sings).

Must-Do

Flip the activity by having students build words from syllables. Using the multisyllabic words from the guided-reading text and other familiar words, make a set of syllable cards and have students combine them into words. They should record their words on a piece of paper to share at the next guided reading lesson.

Learning Goal: Students will be able to word-solve multisyllabic words by breaking them into syllables.

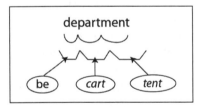

Vocabulary Highlights

Learning Goal: Students will be able to analyze challenging vocabulary.

Developing readers have enough confidence and competence as readers to be able to figure out many new words on their own. This lesson guides students in identifying challenging vocabulary and using word-solving strategies to decipher them.

Instead of telling students to "find three words you have trouble with," I find it sometimes works best to tell students to "find three words that *someone else* might have trouble with."

After reading, have students revisit the text to highlight three tricky words in their reading. Make a list of the words that the students identify. Use context clues, background knowledge, and connections to other words to collaboratively figure out what the words mean. Be sure to have students articulate the strategies they used to solve the meanings of the words.

Must-Do

We need to have several exposures to a word in a variety of contexts to make a word our own. In this routine, students create connections that help them remember new words. This activity can be taught and practiced with the whole class, and used as both a must-do for guided reading and a concept review for other content studies. It's important that this task be modeled and practiced before expecting children to complete it independently.

Vocabulary Squares: Have students choose any two vocabulary words that they would like to remember and create a vocabulary square for each. Use the Four-Square Organizer on Appendix page 159.

1. In the centre diamond, write the word.
2. In the first box, copy the sentence that contains the word from the passage.
3. In the second box, write a definition, either from a dictionary or your own.
4. In the third box, write a personal connection that helps you remember the word.
5. In the fourth box, draw a picture or choose a symbol that helps you remember the word.

Reading with Fluency

Readers Theatre

Learning Goal: Students will be able to read from a script with phrasing and expression.

Readers theatre is a type of dramatic presentation in which players read their roles from scripts, with minimal props and action. All the expression must be conveyed through the voice. It is a great fluency-building activity because it requires readers to rehearse and perform an oral reading passage in groups.

There are many readers theatre scripts available online and through print publications. Some leveled book collections include readers theatre scripts. You can also create your own script from any text, fiction or nonfiction; narratives with plenty of dialogue are most effective.

Choose an appropriately leveled readers theatre script and treat it as any other guided-reading text, with a book introduction, comprehension and word-study focus, and after-reading response. It's important to take time to examine the structure and purpose of a script and how it differs from narrative text.

After reading, talk with students about the characters and how they might speak. Revisit the script to look for cues, such as punctuation, italics, or bold print, that help a reader speak as the character. Talk about how meaning can be conveyed in different ways by emphasizing different words. Read some lines chorally to practice emphasizing words, raising voices, changing tempos, or pausing. Read through the entire script in unison (choral reading can be an excellent fluency-builder) or assign a role to each student.

Must-Do

Have students practice the script introduced in guided reading and present it to the rest of the class as a performance.

Noisy Punctuation

Learning Goal: Students will be able to read orally in phrases.

Help students read in phrases by inserting gestures and sound effects for punctuation as they read aloud. Many years ago, the comedian Victor Borge generated hilarity simply by reading a passage, making strange sounds when there was punctuation in the text—a schtick he called "phonetic punctuation." Your students are likely to find it equally hilarious to blow a raspberry sound and make an exaggerated pointing gesture with their finger when they encounter a period, or produce a little "nrrt" sound with a hook movement of the finger for a comma. But the best part is that they are learning to attend to the signals that indicate when to pause or raise our voices and when to read smoothly in phrases.

You and your students can make up your own sounds and gestures for each punctuation mark—or check out one of the many videos of Victor Borge online to get ideas from him.

Must-Do

Have students work in pairs to prepare a performance reading with sound effects. Ask them to choose an excerpt from a previously read guided-reading text and practice reading it together smoothly, with exaggerated dramatic expression. They'll have so much fun with it they won't even realize that they are learning about fluent reading.

Responding to Reading

In earlier stages, students responded to their reading mainly by talking and drawing. We want developing readers to have plenty of opportunities for talk, but we also want them to do more writing in response to reading. Writing can help readers organize and express their thoughts, supporting both comprehension and retention.

Eventually, most of these students will be expected to write about reading in large-scale assessments. Testing aside, prompted writing is a life skill. The developing reader-writer stage is a good time to introduce the unique skill of responding to an open-ended prompt.

What Is the Question Asking?

Learning Goal: Students will be able to respond to a prompt.

As students begin to prepare for responding to prompts, there are some basic guidelines they need to learn. For example, they must *always* give support from the text, even if the prompt doesn't specifically ask for it. Also, they must be sure to always answer the question "Why do you think so?" or "How do you know?" even if it is not in the prompt.

Often a prompt will ask several things in one question. In this lesson, students learn to analyze the components of a prompt in order to provide complete answers.

When developing reading-related prompts, make sure the question or prompt requires the readers to understand and refer to the passage. A prompt like "What would you have written if you were Sara?" might be addressed quite eloquently without even reading the passage, whereas a prompt like "Do you think Ms Tuddle should have accepted Sara's stories?" requires not only critical and creative thinking, but also an understanding of the story.

> Ms Tuddle has asked the students to write about their favorite things. What do you think Sara will write? Tell why you think so.

Create an open-ended prompt related to the guided reading text. Have students read it and talk about all the things that the prompt asks them to do. Together, highlight key words like "tell why" or "explain." Guide students in collaboratively constructing an effective response that addresses all parts of the prompt and provides evidence from the text. Use a shared- or interactive-writing approach to transfer the ideas to paper. Revisit the response to assess whether it responds completely to the prompt.

Must-Do

Provide students with an open-ended prompt from the guided-reading text and have them write their own responses.

The Reading–Writing Connection

Just as developing writers do not need to devote as much energy to reading individual words as they did in earlier stages, they are also able to write many words automatically or with minimal effort. They enjoy reading longer texts like chapter books and they often want to write longer texts as well. Developing writers can generate many ideas with imaginative and varied content, but those ideas often lack a coherent sequence. It is as if the writer puts thoughts to paper just as they came to mind—a sort of stream-of-consciousness writing. Developing writers need to learn to put their ideas in a logical order, to group details that belong together, and to create a shape to their writing.

Readers at this stage	*Writers at this stage*
• can cope with longer texts; begin to read beginning chapter books • read about topics beyond their personal experience. • read imaginative and realistic fiction as well as nonfiction text forms • read books with choppy sentences and a mechanical voice • attend to the words a writer chooses, and can identify "wow" words • read many words automatically; have more focus on text-level comprehension than word-level; begin to use punctuation in reading and to read in phrases	• can write many details on a topic; enjoy writing longer texts • tend to write ideas in random order; write with a clear topic, which may be beyond their personal experience • independently write in different text forms; might lose their writing voice as they focus on conventions • often write short, choppy sentences or long run-on sentences • begin to experiment with interesting words • demonstrate increasing mastery of spelling and conventions, though they still use readable invented spelling for difficult words

Organizing Ideas

Retelling stories that have been read can help young writers think about how writers organize their ideas. In having them retell a story, we're teaching students to consider beginning, middle, and end; the important events; and the supporting details. Graphic organizers like the 3–2–1 Planner on page 89 are excellent tools for written retellings and can later be used for planning original stories or personal memoirs.

- In the first row, write the title of the book or story you are retelling.
- In the next three boxes, summarize what happened at the beginning, the middle, and the end of the story.
- In the Details boxes, add additional details to each section.

Voice

One of the best ways to teach students to add voice to their writing is to have them take on another point of view, such as that of a story character. Have students write letters from one character to another, such as in this "Dear Three Bears" example written by a Grade 2 student.

> Dear Three Bears,
> I'm sorry because I thought you were downstairs playing pool and you couldn't answer the door. The porridge was good but I thought that you ate already. I am sorry, Baby Bear, that I broke your chair. I thought I would be perfect for the chair. I am sorry for messing your nice house.
> From
> Goldilocks
> —*Olivia*

Combining Sentences

Developing writers are starting to grasp the concept of a *sentence* as a special group of words with a *who* or *what* and an *is* or *does.* Use short sentences from the guided-reading text to review the structure of sentences, and have students practice identifying the subject (name word) and verb (doing word). Many texts at the developing level—both published and by student writers—have too many short sentences, making the writing sound choppy. In this lesson, students will practice combining short sentences using basic conjunctions.

Select sample compound sentences from the guided-reading text that contain the most common conjunctions: *and, but, or, because,* and *so.* Tell students that these are linking words; they link two sentences together. (You might point out that words like *and* and *or* also link groups of words together.)

Create a set of short sentences, preferably from or related to the guided-reading text, and write them on cards; for example

> Sara went shopping. She bought new shoes.
> I ate a hamburger for lunch. I didn't have any fries.
> Do you want to watch TV? Do you want to play a game?

Have students play games by drawing or selecting cards and using linking words to combine the short sentences. Use sticky notes to change capital letters to lower case or delete unnecessary punctuation.

Sample Guided Reading Lesson Plan for Developing Readers

Title	**Learning Goals**
What a Story! Chapters 3–4	Comprehension: asking questions during reading Word Study: chunking three-syllable words Fluency: using punctuation signals

Text/Book Introduction

Preview:

This is a chapter book about a girl named Sara who has lots of trouble thinking of things to write about during writing time in school. So she makes up all kinds of excuses about why she couldn't write a story. Sara has a very good imagination and I think you're going to find some of her excuses really funny. Today we're going to read just a couple of chapters of the book; then you may put it in your book boxes to read the rest of the book on your own.

Prior Knowledge:

An "excuse" is a reason or explanation you give for not doing something you were supposed to do. For example, somebody just said to me last week, "Ms. J, I didn't get my homework done because I had soccer practice after school." That's an excuse – a reason for not doing something. Sometimes you might give an excuse for doing something you weren't supposed to do, like "Mom, I ate the last piece of chocolate cake after school because I was starving and there was no other snack for me." Turn and talk to your partner about when you might have made an excuse or heard someone else make an excuse.

Purpose:

We've been talking a lot about wondering as we read. As you know, good readers wonder all the time, then think about the answers to their wonderings. We know that sometimes our wonderings are answered right there in the book and sometimes we have to figure out the answers in our own heads. Today, as you read, think about your "I wonders." We'll pause every few pages to share our wonderings and try to predict the answers.

Day 1	**Must-Do**
• Book introduction • Vocabulary: *imagine* (Chunk It) • Turn to page 7, Chapter 3 • Stop sign: p 10. *Tab two places where you wondered.* • Record students' wonderings on a chart and invite predictions of answers.	Put Stop signs at the end of chapter 4. *Read this section and tab at least 3 more "wonderings," writing the questions on the sticky tabs.* *Think about the answers to the wonderings.*
Day 2	**Must-Do**
• Review wonderings from the must-do task and add them to chart • Invite students to suggest answers to the wonderings • Code the questions/answers "in the book" (directly answered) or "in my head" (inferred) • Have students reread sections of text independently or in pairs to look for missing answers • Model question cubes	• Buddy work • Question cubes (roll a die with who/what/where/when/why/how and ask a question for the buddy to answer)
Day 3	**Must-Do**
• Three-syllable word chunking (*computer, department, imagine, excuses, hurricane, tornado*) • Fluency work: Noisy Punctuation • Introduce writing prompt	*Written Response: Ms Tuddle has asked the students to write about their favorite things. What do you think Sara will write? Tell why you think so.*

Character Report Card

Character's Name: _____

Teacher's Name: _____

Subject	Always	Usually	Never	No Rating	Comments

Reading Around the Word

Focus Word	Clues from the Text	What I think the Word Means

3-2-1 Planner

Title:

Beginning	Middle	End
Details	*Details*	*Details*

Pembroke Publishers ©2012 *Guiding Readers* by Lori Jamison Rog ISBN 978-1-55138-273-9

6

Guiding Fluent Readers

Jackson's favorite book is the Guinness Book of World Records. *This book is always popular with the boys because of its short chunks of illustrated text and its focus on fascinating facts. Jackson fancies himself something of a walking encyclopedia and hardly a day goes by that he doesn't quote some fascinating fact he's encountered in the* Guinness Book *or another book of trivia. Jackson rarely chooses to read fiction but, when he does, he likes mystery books. He's good at figuring out clues and putting them all together to solve the mystery.*

Like many students in his Grade 3 class, Jackson is considered to be in the fluent stage of reading development, a stage that will last for the rest of his life. Fluent readers can cope with longer words, longer sentences, and longer texts. They are learning not only to be strategic readers, but to be metacognitive as well; that is, to use comprehension strategies deliberately and purposefully to solve reading problems.

In spite of Jackson's competence as a reader right now, however, he is a reader at risk. Too many students lose interest in reading after third grade, a phenomenon known as the "fourth-grade reading slump." Even those who can read choose not to. No one knows exactly why this happens, although experts have attributed it to various causes, such as higher demands of content reading and transitioning from picture books to novels. Jackson presents an additional challenge in that he's a boy. Test data from around the world show that boys score lower than girls in literacy assessments and are less likely to read by choice. That's why it's particularly important for Jackson's teacher to expose him to a variety of genres and forms of reading to find his literacy niche.

Fluent readers

- have a range of strategies for tackling challenging vocabulary
- rarely make miscues that interfere with meaning when reading appropriately leveled text
- can go back into a text to clarify confusion or search for information
- can articulate and use a repertoire of comprehension strategies
- understand that some points of view are different from their own
- can read orally with phrasing, expression, and fluency
- can sustain interest in and attention to longer texts
- can access a wide range of genres and text forms for information and pleasure
- are able to make inferences, evaluations, and interpretations of text
- are beginning to read critically, identifying author's purpose and message

- can summarize the main events in a text

Even at the fluent stage, there are many struggling readers. For example, the Grade 6 student who is reading at Grade 3 level might show many characteristics of fluent readers, but still needs additional intervention if he or she is to function at grade level.

Some teachers assume that fluent-stage readers who are reading at grade level no longer need small-group instruction. They couldn't be more wrong! There are many reasons to provide small-group instruction for readers at and beyond grade level. For one thing, we owe all our students the opportunity to learn and grow as readers, even if they are already reaching grade-level standards. Small-group reading instruction enables us to guide these readers at all stages of development as they process increasingly sophisticated texts. These students may not be well-served by whole-group instruction that focuses on strategies and concepts that do not meet their needs. Small-group reading instruction provides a forum for students to experiment with more complex texts, to talk with others about the content and the reading process, and to extend their reach as readers, writers, and thinkers.

Guided-reading group size for fluent readers can be larger than for younger students, if they are reading at grade level—as many as eight to ten students—and they can meet less frequently. Some teachers blend guided-reading groups with literature circles or reading workshop. (The chart shows a comparison of different grouping structures.) There are different approaches to reading instruction, but the key is for students to be reading accessible texts that support them while stretching them as readers.

> Having students take turns reading an unfamiliar text (the dreaded round-robin reading) doesn't teach anyone to be a better reader. Always give students a chance to prepare before they read publicly.

Small-Group Reading Structures

	Guided Reading	Literature Circles/Discussion Groups	Reading Workshop
Grouping	Groups of 4–8, based on reading levels and/or needs	Groups of 4–8, based on choice and interest in reading a particular text	Individual
Reading Materials	• Matched to instructional level of students, chosen by the teacher • Short texts and excerpts	• Represent a range of reading levels and topics, although they may have a common theme or genre • Students select from a range offered by the teacher • Generally novels, but also can include full-length nonfiction texts	• Self-selected, often with teacher guidance • Full-length novels and other texts
Instructional Focus	Focus on the reader rather than the text; skill and strategy work based on assessed needs of group of students	Focus on the text: content, literary elements, text structure, response	Focus on both the reader (strategies) and the text (content), but tends to be more incidental than systematic
Leadership	Teacher-led	Student-led	Student self-directed, with teacher conferences
Advantages	Provides instructional scaffolding and support at the point of need	Creates opportunity for authentic response to reading and discussion	Builds independence and individual instruction
Disadvantages	Needs-based grouping might not expose students to more complex literature or literary concepts	Does not offer specific strategic reading support	Contact with teacher is brief and less frequent; fewer opportunities to address strategy needs

Each of these structures is assumed to be in addition to whole-class strategic instruction, not in place of it.

Guided reading structures will vary according to the needs of the students and the type of texts they are reading. Fluent readers may be asked to read a short section of text silently and use sticky notes to highlight text features or strategy spots. Only after they have done the first reading will the text be discussed, reread, or analyzed for text features. There are also many ways to build oral reading practice into the guided-reading sequence, but always give students a chance to prepare first, from readers theatre to buddy reading.

Texts for Fluent Readers

Making the reader–text match is more challenging at the fluent stage than at any other, mainly because so much of the equation depends on the reader's background knowledge, vocabulary, interest, and independence. There are leveled books for fluent readers. For readers in Grade 3 and beyond, readability formulas such as Fry or Flesch-Kinkaid provide a starting point for determining the general degree of difficulty. (See chapter 7 for more information on readability.) Because fluent-level texts can range from *Chrysanthemum* to *Hamlet*, finding that just-right match for a particular group of readers can be a challenge.

Fluent texts are longer and more complex than those at previous levels. There are likely to be entire pages of text, with few, if any, illustrations. Here we find figurative language and descriptive prose that is not intended to be taken literally. Concepts are more abstract and require the reader to read between and beyond the lines to interpret them. Long, complex sentences are common.

Texts for fluent readers generally contain

- literary language and challenging vocabulary
- complex storylines that extend over a long period of time
- a range of unique text features
- concepts that might be beyond the reader's immediate experience
- sentences of a variety of lengths, structures, and forms
- entire pages of print

Choose Your Bully by Lori Jamison. Reprinted with permission of High Interest Publishing.

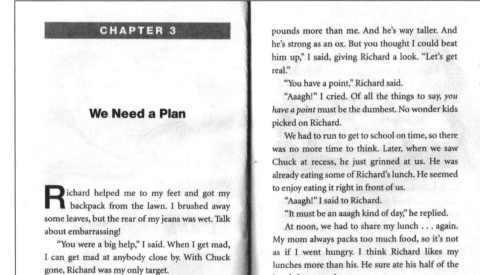

CHAPTER 3

We Need a Plan

Richard helped me to my feet and got my backpack from the lawn. I brushed away some leaves, but the rear of my jeans was wet. Talk about embarrassing!

"You were a big help," I said. When I get mad, I can get mad at anybody close by. With Chuck gone, Richard was my only target.

"I thought you were going to beat him up," Richard said. "You almost did."

"Yeah, right," I told him. "The guy weighs 50 pounds more than me. And he's way taller. And he's strong as an ox. But you thought I could beat him up," I said, giving Richard a look. "Let's get real."

"You have a point," Richard said.

"Aaagh!" I cried. Of all the things to say, *you have a point* must be the dumbest. No wonder kids picked on Richard.

We had to run to get to school on time, so there was no more time to think. Later, when we saw Chuck at recess, he just grinned at us. He was already eating some of Richard's lunch. He seemed to enjoy eating it right in front of us.

"Aaagh!" I said to Richard.

"It must be an aaagh kind of day," he replied.

At noon, we had to share my lunch . . . again. My mom always packs too much food, so it's not as if I went hungry. I think Richard likes my lunches more than his. He sure ate his half of the lunch fast enough.

I tried to get my thoughts together, but I was still too mad. It's hard to think clearly when you're

18

19

The Guided Reading Lesson for Fluent Readers

See page 111 for a sample guided reading lesson plan for fluent readers.

The guided-reading lesson structure for fluent readers is much like that for developing readers. Start with a book introduction that provides a brief overview to establish context, opens up the repertoire of experiences and learning that makes up the students' background knowledge, and guides the reading with an explicitly stated focus or purpose.

Students at this stage will need Reading Toolkits for sticky-note reading (see page 28) and clipboards for writing. They will pause frequently during reading to talk to one another about the text or about their reading processes.

As with developing readers, a general guideline is this:

1. First reading is for general comprehension.
2. Second reading is for comprehension strategy work.
3. Subsequent readings are for vocabulary and word study, fluency work, critical reading, text features, and/or the writer's craft.

Before Reading

Features of the Guided Reading Lesson for Fluent Readers

BEFORE READING
- Book introduction
- Focus on background knowledge

DURING READING
- Silent reading of short sections of text
- Sticky notes to track thinking and record strategies

AFTER READING
- Plenty of discussion of the text and the reading process
- Oral-reading fluency practice built purposefully into the lesson
- Revisiting text for critical reading, higher-level thinking
- Examining writer's craft and literary elements
- Writing in response to reading

An effective book introduction is designed to ensure that readers will have enough strategic independence to cope with the text on their own with some reading work. Sometimes the book introduction will entail building background knowledge, particularly for nonfiction text.

Fluent-level texts are likely to contain some vocabulary unfamiliar to the students. Whether or not we preteach a few words will depend on how critical those words are to understanding the story and how much text support there is for solving the words independently. Fluent readers will be able to decode most of the words they encounter, but they may not always understand the meanings of those words. And equally problematic are familiar words used in different ways. Learning about multiple meanings of words is one of the challenges of fluent reading.

As in other stages of development, the book introduction also sets a purpose for reading. For fluent readers, this purpose might be related to individual comprehension strategies: reading to connect, to wonder, to infer, for example. Often, however, we want to use the guided reading lesson for overall processing of text, so the purpose for reading might be more general: reading to get information about spiders, reading to find out how the character solves the problem, or reading to learn how to make a snowflake, for example.

During Reading

During the guided reading lesson, fluent readers read short sections of text silently to themselves, sometimes using sticky notes to track points of interest or strategy spots. I predetermine the pause points and we place a sticky-note Stop sign on the page to indicate how far to read. At each pause point, we stop to discuss the text and the reading process. There is plenty of talk incorporated into the reading; it's important for readers to be able to articulate their reading processes and their responses to the text.

Reading short sections of text enables us to analyze the strategies students use when they encounter difficulties, to clarify possible confusions in vocabulary and concepts, and to teach young readers to synthesize; that is, to be aware of how their thinking evolves and changes as they read. As the teacher, I always prepare some guiding questions or prompts but, as much as possible, I want the students to generate natural and authentic conversations about the text.

After Reading

The first independent reading of a text enables readers to negotiate the print and get the gist of the passage. Subsequent readings lend themselves to greater fluency, deeper thinking, and more-sophisticated responses. At this stage, we begin to focus on critical reading, analyzing author's purpose, bias, and point of view. We also consider the writer's craft: What techniques has this writer used to convey his/her message? How can we use these techniques in our own writing? We take a close look at figurative language and other literary techniques.

Because students are reading silently, it's important to intentionally build oral-reading fluency practice into the guided-reading sequence. We might have students read the text in pairs, share favorite sections with the group, or rehearse readings for performance in the group. Fluency does not have to be a special event, however. Any time we ask a student to read the section of the text that supports a particular response or to read an interesting fact aloud, we are supporting fluency development.

Must-dos will often involve written responses or further reading, either from the guided-reading text or from other texts. When providing a new text to practice focus strategies, it's important to make sure that the text is at an accessible reading level for the students.

The fluent stage lasts throughout school and throughout life. The guided-reading structure will vary according to the purpose and instructional focus, but always we are supporting students as they work with increasingly sophisticated text.

Sample Areas of Focus

Metacognitive Use of Comprehension Strategies

- Making connections to background knowledge and experience
- Asking questions to clarify and guide thinking
- Drawing inferences
- Generating ongoing predictions based on information in the text, and confirming or adapting them based on further reading
- Generating mental images
- Summarizing
- Monitoring comprehension and using fix-up strategies to clarify
- Synthesizing information
- Reading critically for author's purpose and bias, and for support for opinions
- Identifying main idea, supporting details, author's message and theme
- Interpreting information presented visually, textually, or quantitatively (i.e., charts, graphs, timelines) and being aware of how the information relates to the text
- Understanding a variety of text forms, text structures, and genres

Flexible and Integrated Use of Word-Solving Strategies

- Applying knowledge of nonstandard vowel combinations (e.g., *ea* in *great*)
- Using morphological chunks (prefixes, suffixes, and unfamiliar root words)
- Using signal words to indicate definitional support (e.g., *such as, in other words*)
- Using known word-parts to support understanding of unknown words
- Interpreting words with multiple meanings
- Identifying and interpreting figurative language
- Consulting reference materials (print and digital) to clarify meaning, spelling, and/or pronunciation

Fluent Reading with Appropriate Pacing, Phrasing, Clarity, and Expression

- Attending to less familiar punctuation forms: colon, semi-colon, dash
- Reading aloud with attention to pacing, volume, enunciation
- Reading silently at different rates for different purposes; e.g., scanning for details or skimming for general impression
- Reading poetry, dramatic scripts, narratives, and informational texts with appropriate expression and phrasing

Responding to Reading

- Providing thorough and insightful responses to a prompt
- Offering support from the text when giving explanations, interpretations, or personal responses, quoting directly from the text when appropriate
- Offering evaluative and affective remarks about the content or craft of the writing
- Comparing and contrasting content, characters, and style of two or more different texts
- Summarizing what was read
- Identifying and comparing genres and text structures
- Recognizing and interpreting figurative language and other literary techniques
- Reading critically, analyzing author's purpose and style
- Analyzing elements of the writer's craft and applying them to student writing

Lesson Routines

Comprehension Strategies

Probably the single best way to engage students in active reading and to make them aware of the strategies they are using is to have them track their thinking with sticky notes as they read. Make sure each student has a Reading Toolkit stocked with sticky notes for the lesson. (For instructions on making a Reading Toolkit, see page 28).

Break up the reading of the text into manageable chunks of one to three pages (depending on the amount of print on the page). Have students place their sticky-note Stop signs at the stopping point and read the section of text silently, using sticky notes to track their strategy use, as directed. Stop after each section of reading to have students discuss their thinking, then continue the process with additional sections of text. This talk time is particularly important. When students are required to describe their strategy use for someone else, it helps them clarify and solidify their own thinking—these are important steps on the way to developing metacognitive awareness of the reading process.

For independent learning—the must-do—have students continue to read the same text or provide a new text at their independent-reading levels. Students continue to read, tabbing their strategy spots as they did during the lesson. During the guided reading lesson itself, I rarely have students write on the sticky notes. Because they are reading only short sections of text and discussing their strategies immediately after reading, it isn't usually necessary to have a written record of their ideas. Besides, we want to use as much of this time as possible for reading and talking. But when students continue their strategy work during the must-do, they should record their ideas on the sticky notes. It might be two or three days before the group meets again, so students should have a written record of their thinking during reading.

Coding Connections

Learning Goal: Students will be able to articulate connections they make during reading and identify how these connections support their comprehension.

At earlier stages, students have learned to make connections to their own personal experiences (text to self) and to other readings (text to text). At the fluent stage, we want students to connect to wider knowledge of the world (text to world) as well. Text-to-world connections might be based on big ideas, such as pollution or poverty or friendship, or they might be based on current events in the world, such as the Olympics or a weather disaster. In this lesson, students practice tracking their connections during reading and then coding the connections according to the type of connection.

Choose a text that is likely to generate a range of connections for the students, particularly text-to-world connections. Introduce the text and review the three kinds of connections that readers make. Tell students that during reading they are to use sticky notes to tab two or three places where they made connections to something that they have experienced, read, or learned about in the world. When they tab a connection spot, they should stop and consider what type of connection it is and label the sticky note with *T–S*, *T–T*, or *T–W*.

Connecting to Background Knowledge and Experience

T–S   Text to Self
T–T   Text to Text
T–W   Text to World

Have students read to the designated pause point. When everyone has read the section, have them turn and talk to a partner about the kinds of connections they made. Guide a group discussion about ways in which these connections helped (or sometimes didn't help) the readers understand the text. After the discussion, continue the process with other short sections of text.

Must-Do

Have students read another section of the same text (or a different text at an accessible reading level). They should tab three to five connections and write these connections directly on the sticky notes, to be discussed at the next guided reading lesson. You may want to use color-coded stickies to distinguish the three different types of connections.

At the next guided reading lesson, invite students to share their connections. Have a piece of chart paper available for students to post their stickies. With students, take note of the types of connections used most and which connections were most helpful to understanding the text.

3-H Questions

Learning Goal: Students will be able to self-question as they read and identify how this process supports their own comprehension.

Good readers wonder as they read. Their wonderings help clarify meaning, guide their thinking, and set purposes for reading on. In earlier stages, students learned to think about "in the book" (literal) and "in my head" (inferential) wonderings.

In this lesson, they think about "in my heart" (evaluative or affective) questions as well. This awareness is important, first and foremost, as a reading strategy, but it also can support students in answering questions on assessments. If they can identify a question as *hand*, *heart*, or *head*, it will help them decide how to find the answer. Identifying questions as *hand*, *heart*, and *head* (or literal, evaluative, and inferential) helps students develop metacognition as readers as they recognize the different ways that we access information when we read.

Types of Questions

Hand questions are answered right there in the text.

Head questions are answered by combining clues in the text with what you already know.

Heart questions are answered from your own knowledge and feelings.

Remind students of the importance of wondering as they read. Review the different kinds of wonderings and help students make the connection between wonderings and questions. Sometimes wonderings are answered right there in the text. We call these *hand* questions, because we can put our hand right on the information in the book. Sometimes our wonderings aren't answered in the text, but we can figure out the answer because the author gives us clues. We call these *head* questions because we get the answers by combining our own ideas with those of the author. And sometimes, the author doesn't give us any clues at all, and we just have to figure out the answer from our own background knowledge and experience. We call those *heart* questions because the answers come from inside of us.

Have students use three sticky tabs from their Reading Toolkit. As they read the first section of text, have them tab two or three places where they wondered something. At the end of the reading, have them stop and TTYN (Talk To Your Neighbor) about their wonderings. Ask partners to predict what they think the answers to their wonderings might be. Have students return to the group and share the wonderings and possible answers. Record the students' wonderings on a sheet of chart paper. Where possible, code the wonderings with the symbols for hand, heart, and head. (They won't always know whether there are clues in the text until they read on.)

Have students read on to another section of text, this time looking for answers to their previous wonderings, but also tabbing two or three new wonderings as they read. Repeat the discussion and recording of questions. It might be necessary to go back and change some of the codes if answers or clues to the wonderings were found in the next section of text.

Must-Do

For independent practice, have students read on in the same guided-reading text or from an independent-level text (of student's choice or provided by the teacher) and tab at least four wonderings in the text. Have students record four of their wonderings and their predictions of the answers on a foldable-flap book (see page 161 in Appendix) or the graphic organizer on page 115.

Asking Questions

Learning Goal: Students will be able to generate and answer literal, inferential, and evaluative questions.

Students are accustomed to having the teacher ask questions for them to answer. Now it's their turn to ask the questions. This lesson is a follow-up to The 3-H Questions. When Taffy Raphael (Raphael & Au, 2006) developed the QAR strategy, she focused not just on answering questions but also on examining the relationship between questions and answers; in other words, the process of finding the answers. Helping students identify questions as *hand, heart,* or *head* enables them to understand the processes they must follow to answer those questions.

When we have students answer the questions, we should always be sure to require them to go back into the text to find the evidence or support for the answers.

After reading, have students practice creating questions and identifying them as *hand, heart,* or *head* questions. The chart below offers some guidelines for questioning. Your students will find it very easy to come up with *hand* questions and not too difficult to generate *heart* questions. But inferential *head* questions are tricky (even for teachers) because there must be some clues in the text to help figure out the answer.

Hand Questions • Literal-level questioning • Answers can be found directly in the text	Examples *Who was…?* *When did…?* *What is…?* *Where did…?*
Head Questions • Inferential • There will be clues in the text but the reader must also draw on background knowledge • May be referred to as interpreting, inferring, predicting, concluding	Examples *Why do you think…?* *What do you predict…?* *How do you know…?*
Head Questions • Evaluative or affective • No clues in the text; answers come from reader's own background knowledge or feelings • Often opinion questions	Examples *What would you do if…?* *What do you think the character should do?* *Which do you think is better?*

Must-Do

Creating inferential questions is not easy. Your students will need plenty of guided practice before they can tackle this task on their own.

Have students practice generating questions to bring back to the group. You might ask them to write one of each type of question on an index card, identifying the type of questions and writing the answers on the back of the card. During the next guided reading lesson, students in the group can take turns drawing cards and trying to answer each other's questions.

The Inference Equation

Learning Goal: Students will be able to identify inferences in their reading and explain the textual clues and background knowledge required to make those inferences.

When we combine what we read with what we already know in our background knowledge, we come up with new ideas and interpretations that are not directly stated in the text. That is the inference equation. For example, what can we infer from a simple statement like this: "Sue blew out the candles and opened her presents"? Well, we read that there were candles and presents. We know that people often blow out candles and open presents on their birthdays. So we can infer that it must be Sue's birthday, even though this fact is not stated directly. Obviously, inferences have different levels of complexity. But starting with simple inferences helps students understand the thinking processes involved.

> **What you read + What you know = What you infer**

Even young readers draw inferences all the time. But for strategic readers, it's not enough just to make inferences; we want them to be cognizant of their inferences and the processes that enable them to make those inferences. That is what metacognition is all about. When readers understand what they have done when they make an automatic inference, they will be better able to use the inferring process when they hit a problem in their reading. This is a good follow-up lesson to the 3-H Questions routine because *head* questions require readers to make inferences.

Choose a small section of the guided-reading text that involves a simple inference, such as this sentence from *Baseball Bats* by Sharon Jennings: "Simon is a pretty good pitcher, but he acts like his hand is made of glass." Talk with students about what this sentence means and what kinds of background knowledge a reader needs in order to understand it.

What we read	What we know	What we infer
"Simon is a pretty good pitcher, but he acts like his hand is made of glass."	- a pitcher is the person on a baseball team who throws the ball to the batter - glass breaks easily	Simon acts like his hand could break easily.

Comic Strip Inferences on page 123 provides additional practice in using the inferring process to access humor.

Continue to work with short excerpts directly from the guided-reading text, guiding the students as they draw inferences and support their thinking with clues from the text. Collaboratively complete the inference chart as you read, so that students see their thinking on paper. It's often difficult for young readers to recognize when they've drawn an inference, so start by choosing sections of text that lend themselves to inferring. As students become proficient at identifying their inferences as they read, they can be asked to tab inference spots with sticky notes during reading.

Must-Do

Select three or four pause points in another section of the guided-reading text or in a new independent-level text. Have students place large sticky notes in these designated pause points before reading. As a must-do, students read the passage independently. As they come to a sticky tab, they should note what inference they made. After reading, have students complete a three-column chart (Inference Chart on page 112) by recording what the text said (directly quoting a sentence or phrase), what background knowledge they need to apply, and what inference they drew. Note that sometimes the inference will come first and students will have to reflect back on the textual clues and background knowledge. You may want to have students read and complete the chart in pairs so that they talk through the process as well as writing.

Clicks and Clunks

Learning Goal: Students will be able to identify points of confusion in their reading and use strategies to repair their comprehension.

When our reading is going well, and we understand everything we read, it all just *clicks*. But sometimes in our reading, we hit a *clunk*—something that we just don't understand or that doesn't make sense. Good readers hit clunks all the time. But good readers know when they've hit a clunk and use their strategies to fix it up. Janet Klingner and Sharon Vaughn came up with the language of "clicks and clunks" in their Collaborative Strategic Reading model (1999).

Use a sentence from the guided-reading text to model for students how you might hit a clunk in your reading; for example, "The cowboy rode away on his house." Talk with students about the importance of recognizing when our reading doesn't make sense, then taking time to draw on our strategies to fix up the mix-up.

Choose a guided-reading text that is certain to present just a few clunks for the students. Provide students with a collection of red and green sticky flags in their Reading Toolkits. Tell students to read a designated section of text. When they encounter a problem (a clunk), they should tab it with a red flag, to indicate that they had a breakdown in comprehension. However, if they are able to use a fix-up strategy to make sense of the text, they should replace the red flag with a green flag, to show that they corrected the confusion. If they can't fix the confusion, they leave the red flag and read on.

After everyone has read the section of text, stop and talk about the spot or spots where the students hit clunks. (It's likely to be the same place for most of the students in the group.) Discuss what fix-up strategies the students used and what other strategies they might use another time.

Continue reading sections of text in this way for the rest of the guided-reading time.

Must-Do

Have students read on in the same text or provide them with an independent-level text to read. (You might manipulate an existing text by retyping it and inserting deliberate errors or confusions.) Have students tab any points of confusion—often it is necessary to say something like, "I think you will hit at least three clunks in this text"—with red and/or green flags. During the next guided reading session, discuss their points of confusion and how they might use strategies to get those clunks clicking again.

Synthesizing

Synthesis is the most sophisticated of the reading strategies. It refers to the way our thinking evolves as we read new information. For example, when we make a prediction during reading, then change our prediction as we read, we are synthesizing—changing our thinking to accommodate new information. Tanny McGregor (2007) uses Russian stacking dolls as a metaphor to explain synthesis. Just as the dolls grow each time we add a new one on top, our thinking expands each time we add a new bit of understanding from our reading.

Choose a guided-reading text that lends itself to evolving thinking, such as one with a character who changes or a surprise plot direction. Plan two or three strategic pause points to stop and discuss what's happening in the text.

Introduce the text and have students read the first section independently. After they have read it, have them talk with a partner and/or with the group about what they are thinking. You might need to prompt them with questions about the character or the storyline. Then have the students read on in the same text and talk about how their thinking has changed—and what information in the text made them change their thinking. Continue this process with guiding questions and prompting to extend their thinking and provide support from the text for their ideas. Together, complete a Synthesizing Chart graphic organizer (see page 112).

I love the use of the term *clunks* to refer to a break down in comprehension, because it makes the process more concrete and takes away the stigma of calling something a mistake.

Remote-Control Reading on page 124 is another self-monitoring routine that reminds students to stop and think about whether their reading is making sense.

Learning Goal: Students will be able to explain how their thinking evolves as they add new layers of meaning from their reading.

Encouraging students to be aware of how their thinking changes during reading is an important reading strategy. This lesson requires carefully crafted questions and sensitive prompting to guide children in thinking about their strategies.

As with all comprehension strategies, this should be practiced in guided reading only after students have had exposure to and experience with the language of synthesis through read-alouds and shared reading.

Must-Do

Provide students with a three-column graphic organizer and a couple of short passages of independent-level text. Have them record their interpretation at the beginning and at the end of the reading, and what information in the reading made them change their thinking. Having students work in pairs on this activity can generate important dialogue as the students negotiate what to write on the chart.

Predict and Confirm

Learning Goal: Students will be able to make credible predictions about what will happen in the text, then use text clues to confirm or adjust their predictions as they read.

Predicting is a form of synthesis. Good readers are constantly predicting what will happen in their texts, then adjusting or confirming their predictions based on what they read. Inviting students to make a prediction based on the cover of a book, then waiting until the book is done to revisit that prediction, doesn't really contribute much to strategic understanding. We want our students to be constantly revising their predictions as they read, using new information that they read.

This routine is very similar to the Synthesizing lesson on page 100. Choose a guided-reading text that lends itself to adjusting predictions two or three times. Plan pause points for revisiting predictions during reading. To make an educated prediction, the reader needs to have a little background knowledge. That's why I don't have students make predictions until we've read the first section of text.

Have students read independently to the first pause point, and turn and talk with a partner about what they think is going to happen next in the text. In some cases, you might offer a question or prompt: *What do you think the character is going to do next? How do you think this problem will be solved?* This often helps generate deeper thinking and richer dialogue. It's important that students explain their predictions with direct support from the text.

Continue reading to the next pause point. Repeat the process, with students talking to their partners about whether they will stand by their original predictions or change their predictions. Many students need to be convinced that it's okay to change their predictions. In fact, authors often deliberately set up readers to think in a certain way, only to surprise us with a twist in the plot. Recall the stacking dolls in the previous routine: as we read, our thinking gets bigger and often looks a little bit different.

Must-Do

Use the same process as with The Inference Equation routine on page 98. Provide students with an accessible text (preferably at their independent-reading level) and have them place two or three large sticky notes at pre-selected pause points. As they read independently, they should stop when they come to the first sticky note to record their predictions and reasons for their predictions. Then they read on, and when they come to the second sticky note, they record their new predictions and support. If they are repeating their original prediction, they should indicate what information in the new section of text supports the original prediction. At the next guided reading lesson, invite students to share their predictions, reinforcing the use of textual information rather than the correctness of the predictions.

Rainbow Strategy Spots

Learning Goal: Students will be able to identify the strategies they use as they read.

Although we sometimes work on one strategy at a time during guided reading, actual reading rarely involves applying just one strategy. We want fluent readers to be able to access a range of strategies, flexibly and purposefully, according to the demands of a particular reading situation. This lesson helps them identify and articulate the strategies they use as they read. This routine can be done with any group of strategies, although I like to start with connecting, questioning, and inferring. Identify each strategy with its own color of sticky tab.

Provide students with a rich guided-reading text and a collection of different-colored sticky tabs in their Reading Toolkits (see page 28). As they read each section of text, students track their thinking by tabbing strategy points with the appropriate color. For example, if they wondered something, they should tab the spot where they wondered with a yellow sticky; if they made a connection, they should tab the spot with a pink sticky; and if they drew an inference, they should tab the spot with an orange sticky. After reading a section of text, students turn and talk about what strategies they used. Continue with additional sections of text, as long as the guided-reading time permits.

You can display a sheet of chart paper divided into three columns, each labeled with a strategy. Have students place their sticky notes in the appropriate column. Talk about which strategies appear most often and why that might be. Invite students to set goals for which strategies they need to develop.

Must-Do

Often, deeper comprehension emerges only on repeated reading. You might have students go back and reread the same section of text and tab different strategies this time. During must-do reading, they record their thinking about connections, questions, or inferences directly on the sticky tabs. At the next guided reading lesson, discuss the new rainbows of stickies and invite students to share how their reading process was different on the second reading.

Word-Solving Strategies

Morphological chunks include root words; inflectional endings (such as -*ing* or -*ed*) that indicate tense, plurality, comparison, or part of speech; prefixes and suffixes added to the beginning or end of a root word to change the meaning of the word (such as *re-* or -*less*). Other structural analysis elements include compound words, possessives, and contractions.

Fluent readers recognize many words at sight or with minimal decoding. Even when a word is challenging, sounding it out isn't usually very helpful at this stage. Fluent readers can usually pronounce most words; the problem is that they don't always know what the words mean. There are three main ways that fluent readers solve unfamiliar words: using context clues; breaking the word into chunks; and, when all else fails, consulting an external reference such as a dictionary or another person. In chapter 5, we practiced using context clues or "reading around the word" and chunking words into syllables or rimes. Probably the most useful strategy for multisyllabic words is breaking down the word into chunks of meaning or morphological segments.

Patricia Cunningham's Nifty Thrifty Fifty is a list of fifty anchor words representing all the most common prefixes and suffixes. A color-coded list of these words can be found at www.teachers.net/4blocks/frazierNifty ThriftyFifty.doc.

Patricia Cunningham (1998) believes that readers can use root words and affixes to solve unfamiliar words, not necessarily by knowing the meanings of the various units (whether recognizably English or Latin or Greek) but by connecting them to known words. She calls this *phonics by analogy*. According to Cunningham, the brain is not a rule-follower, but a pattern-finder. Readers are taught to notice patterns in words and apply what they know about these familiar patterns to solve other words; for example, if *redo* means "do again," then *reread* probably means "read again."

Chunk and Link

Learning Goal: Students will be able to apply analogies to chunks of familiar words in order to solve unfamiliar words.

Small-group guided reading is an excellent time to reinforce knowledge of patterns and chunks as a word-solving strategy, because students can apply this strategy in the context of connected reading. In this lesson they will learn how to look for chunks of meaning, such as prefixes, suffixes, and root words (also known as stem or base words). Linking those chunks to known words can help readers figure out the meanings of unfamiliar words.

Provide students with several pieces of highlighting tape and have them scan their guided-reading text for words that have prefixes and/or suffixes. This might be completed as an independent learning must-do rather than in guided-reading time.

Record the students' words on a piece of chart paper. Have students interactively chunk the words by circling the prefixes and suffixes. Together, try to come up with a familiar word that contains each prefix to link to the unfamiliar word. Using the analogy to a familiar word, as well as the students' own background knowledge, collaboratively construct a possible definition for the multisyllabic words.

Word	Context	Root word	Link words	What the chunk means	What the new word might mean
disagreeable	*How could one sister be so kind and the other so disagreeable?*	agree	disappear believable	• *Dis-* means "not" • *able*	Not able to agree; arguing, unpleasant
unhappiest	*She was the unhappiest, grumpiest princess anyone had ever seen.*	happy	untie smartest	• *Un-* means "not"; if your shoes are untied, they are not tied. • *-est* means "most"	• not happy • the most sad or angry
ripening	*We watched our pumpkins ripening on the vine.*	ripe	tightening	• When you add *-en* to a word, you cause it become, like to make a knot tight	Becoming ripe

Must-Do

Have students work in pairs to continue the chart with the remaining words from the list, or hunt for additional words from the text.

Reading with Fluency

Robot Reading and Opera Reading

Learning Goal: Students will be able to read a text orally with appropriate expression and tone.

Many lessons and tips for developing oral reading fluency can be found in the chapters on developing readers and struggling readers. Most fluent-level readers are now reading in phrases rather than word by word. This is particularly important as they encounter longer and longer sentences in their reading. If readers are still reading dysfluently, it can be a big impediment to navigating the long, complex sentences we often find in fluent-level text; however, many otherwise-fluent readers still read aloud without appropriate expression or even in monotone. A fun way to get students rereading a text for fluency practice is to use different voices and reading styles.

Choose a section of guided-reading text that lends itself to expressive reading, such as dialogue. Read it together, in chorus, in *robot reading*; that is, flat and expressionless. Then read the same section of text together in *opera reading*, overly dramatic reading with exaggerated expression. Finally, have students practice with a partner reading the same text with natural and appropriate expression that conveys the meaning of the text.

Must-Do

A silly voice can be like a mask—it gives the reader something to hide behind so he or she doesn't have to be exposed in public. Provide each pair of students with an engaging piece of short text, such as a poem, to practice reading in silly voices, then perform for the group at the next guided reading session.

Skim, Scan, or Skip?

We read at different rates and in different ways for different purposes. Sometimes we need to read slowly, or *walk* through the text, especially when the text contains lots of information or difficult reading. Sometimes we *jog* through a text, such as recreational reading of an easy novel. And sometimes we *run* through the text, especially when we need to skim for an overview of the text or scan the page quickly for specific information.

> **Tools of Quick Reading**
>
> **Skimming**: running your eyes quickly over the page to get the general gist or main idea of the text
> **Scanning**: running your eyes quickly over the page to find specific information
> **Skipping**: ignoring text that doesn't meet your purpose for reading

Remind students of the three tools of quick reading. Starting with skimming, talk with students about when and why readers might skim a text. We skim when we want a quick overview of the text and don't need all the details. Often we will skim a page or two of a book to decide if we might want to read it more carefully. Start with a piece of independent-level (easy-peasy) text. Display a paragraph of four to six lines, one line at a time, at a moderate rate. Ask students to TTYN (Talk To Your Neighbor) about what the text is about. Try another paragraph, a little more quickly. Gradually increase the amount of text until students are reading a whole paragraph at once, running their eyes quickly over the print, and can summarize in a few words what the paragraph is about.

When students demonstrate that they can skim and summarize the text, work on scanning. We scan when we want to find a specific piece of information or detail. Display a page of text from a familiar or easy guided-reading text. Ask students a detail question; e.g., Where was the boy going? or How large do snails grow? The students must run their eyes quickly over the page to find the information. Gradually increase the complexity of the question and the length of the text students must scan.

Finally, skipping is the easiest strategy. If you're looking for information about the size of the snail, you don't need to scan the section on what snails eat. You can skip that section. Nonfiction text often helps us by giving us subheads. But even in fiction, you know you will be able to skip some parts if they don't suit your

---

Learning Goal: Students will be able to demonstrate different reading styles and rates for different purposes.

Today's technology can be a great asset in providing practice with quick reading. Using an interactive whiteboard or data projector, flash the text up quickly, line by line. However, even with print on paper, students can practice quick reading by running a ruler under lines of printed text.

purpose for reading. Provide a prompt or question and talk with students about how they can decide which sections of the text to scan and which to skip.

Must-Do

Twenty Questions in Twenty Minutes: Provide students with a series of questions for which they must skim text for the answers. Make the questions quite simple and the answers short—one or two words. The key is to find the answer, not necessarily to think critically or creatively. See how many questions they can answer correctly in the time frame provided. You might have students record the page numbers as well as the answers.

Responding to Reading

Just as texts become increasingly more sophisticated as readers progress through the fluent-reader stage, so do expectations for student responses to reading. Rather than simply retelling what they've read, students are expected to summarize, a more cognitively demanding task that requires them to analyze, prioritize, and synthesize what they have read. We guide our students as they analyze the texts for figurative language, literary devices, and elements of the writer's craft. We require them to respond to what's on the lines, what's between the lines, and what's beyond the lines. Critical reading is beyond-the-lines reading. It requires readers to be aware of not just what is said, but also how it is said and why it is said—a demanding but essential skill for today's literacies.

Summarizing

Learning Goal: Students will be able to summarize key points in a text.

When early readers retell what they have read, they are asked to relay every single detail of the text, regardless of its level of importance. In the chapter on developing readers, we worked on separating a retelling into general statements (beginning, middle, end) and supporting details. Now that our students are fluent readers, we want them to master the sophisticated skill of summarizing. Summarizing requires readers to restate, combine, organize, and paraphrase what they've read.

> **Some Rules for Summarizing**
> 1. Make sure to include all information that is important.
> 2. Leave out information that's not important (extra details).
> 3. Put the information in order.
> 4. Don't repeat information, even if it's repeated in the text.
> 5. Use category words instead of lists of words (e.g. *food* instead of *carrots, cookies, and milk*).
> 6. Combine ideas or events that go together.
> 7. Use your own words, except for important words from the text.

Instruction and practice in summarizing improves students' overall comprehension of text content. (Duke & Pearson, 2002)

Use a shared-writing approach (i.e., composing the text together while the teacher scribes) to summarize a short guided-reading text that has been previously read. It's helpful to display the text using a document projector or other tool. Together with students, analyze the text sentence by sentence. Talk about what information is important and what is merely interesting. Discuss which ideas can be combined together in one sentence. Together, compose a summary that pulls all the information together.

Must-Do

Students will need plenty of practice in a guided setting before you can expect them to write summaries on their own. Until students are ready to tackle independent summaries, you might want to provide them with a simple framework, such as the one on page 113.

Active Bookmarks

Active bookmarks are a set of strategy-based sentence stems that require students to think about their reading processes. Each bookmark requires the reader to reflect on a different action or reading process, such as character analysis, inference, or visualization. Eight different bookmarks are provided on page 114. It's best to ensure that students master one or two at a time. However, working with them is quite easy and simply reinforces strategies that have already been taught and practiced.

Introduce each bookmark by generating responses together, so that students know what an adequate response sounds like. Prepare a set of bookmarks—several copies of only two or three strategies to start with—and turn the bookmarks face down on the table. Have students reread a designated page or excerpt from their guided-reading text. After reading, each student chooses a bookmark at random and must TTYN (Talk To Your Neighbor), responding to the prompt on his or her bookmark. If two partners get the same prompt, one must elaborate on the other's response. After they practice in partners, you might have students share with the whole group. This gives you a chance to probe students' responses and to invite others to elaborate or extend the responses.

Must-Do

Have each student draw two or three bookmarks and insert them in random places into his/her guided-reading text. Students must complete the written response on the bookmark using the information in the section where the bookmark landed (see sample below).

> The character __Zach__ reminds me of
> __Lots-o in Toy Story__ because
> he pretends to be nice but then he's mean to the other kids.

Critical Reading

Critical readers are able to read beyond what the author says to how and why the author says it. Critical reading shows us ways of looking at texts to recognize, question, and challenge the attitudes, values, and beliefs that lie beneath the surface of the writing. There are three main components to critical reading: identifying the author's purpose; understanding tone and techniques; and recognizing bias.

The critical reader asks questions like these: What does the author expect from the reader—to be entertained, informed, amused, persuaded? Are there any tools and techniques the author has used to achieve his or her purpose—language, organization, text structure, formatting, text features? Authors use italics, bold print, ellipses, and visuals for specific purposes. Readers need be aware of them and to know why they are used.

An important purpose of critical reading is to recognize the author's point of view. Does the author have a particular bias? Is the writing factual or opinion-based? Does the author provide a balanced argument or emphasize (or ignore) evidence to support his or her opinion?

These are the kinds of questions we can be asking students—and teaching them to ask themselves—as we build the habits of critical readers. As always, as we ask guiding questions, we want to prompt students to support their answers with evidence from the text as well as from their own background experience. Here is a list of prompts for helping students think critically:

- How do the pictures and other graphics help you understand the information in the text?
- How do you think the author wants us as readers to feel or respond when we read this?
- Why do you think the author used this particular visual/detail/text feature/ print feature in this place?
- Are there any voices or points of view missing from this text? If so, what are they?
- Is there any information missing that would make this reading clearer for you?
- Does this text represent the topic fairly?
- Do you agree with the author's point of view? If not, why do you think differently?
- What is the message or lesson the author wants us to take away as readers?
- Can you think of other texts that also present a similar message? Does this text present the message as well as or better than other texts?
- Is there information presented here that you're not sure is accurate or true?

Must-Do

Choose one or more of the critical reading questions and have students complete a written response.

The Reading–Writing Connection

At this stage, we expect a certain mastery of basic conventions, such as capital letters, end-of-sentence punctuation, subject–verb agreement, and spelling of grade-appropriate words. But we need to recognize that these students are still novice writers, even in intermediate grades and beyond. The more risks students take with vivid vocabulary, the more likely they are to misspell complex words. The more they try to write long, flowing sentences, the more likely they are to make mistakes in grammar or punctuation. As teachers, we walk a fine line between setting standards for correctness and encouraging risk-taking and experimentation. In many cases, a more sophisticated piece of writing may very well have more errors in conventions than a less creative piece.

Not having to write every word letter by letter frees up the memory to focus more on the craft of writing. Students can hold longer stories in their heads and elaborate more on details. We want to encourage our students to read as writers as well as readers, to pay attention to how a writer has crafted a sentence or used an interesting turn of phrase.

Readers at this stage	Writers at this stage
• read texts of increasing length and complexity	• write texts of increasing length and complexity; can generate rich details, elaboration, and description
• can identify and access different types of text structures	• use a variety of text forms for different purposes; plan and organize ideas for logical structure, with leads and conclusions
• are beginning to consider author's purpose, message, and point of view when reading	• begin to consider audience and purpose when writing
• understand and appreciate figurative language and literary techniques	• use more vivid vocabulary and "book language," such as figures of speech
• read with increasing fluency	• use resources such as thesaurus or dictionary
• can process longer, more complex sentences	• generate longer, more complex sentences
• read most words automatically; use a range of cueing systems to solve unfamiliar words	• spell many words conventionally but still may use phonetic spelling for difficult words
• use punctuation, paragraphing, and other text supports to aid comprehension	• usually use capitals and basic punctuation correctly

Notice It! Name It! Try It!

One of the unique features of fluent-level text is the use of figurative language and literary devices. The Techniques Writers Use anchor chart (see sample below) invites readers to identify interesting elements of the writer's craft. When we notice an interesting turn of phrase, we record it on the chart and collaborate to give it a name that is meaningful for the students. There is power in students labeling the technique themselves because, when they name it, they "own" it. And students are more likely to use the technique in their own writing. It's your choice whether or not introduce the official name, such as *alliteration* instead of *sound words*, but this is most effectively taught after students have constructed their own understanding of the technique and given it a try themselves. You can maintain a classroom anchor chart of Techniques Writers Use (see page 115 for template) for all the students to access during writing.

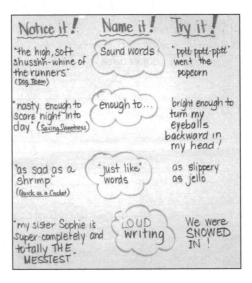

Sentence Stretching

Students at the fluent stage are reading longer, more flowing sentences and start to experiment with crafting more fluent sentences as well. Sentence Stretching invites young writers to add descriptive words and phrases to make sentences more interesting and fluid. Provide students with a sentence from their guided-reading text that is full of interesting details and sounds rhythmical to the ear, such as this sentence from Sylvia McNicol's *Tiger Catcher's Kid* (Nelson, 1989):

> She stood there for a minute in her towelly robe, with her hair standing at attention like little spikes or antennae.

Talk about the basic core of the sentence, the subject and verb, which are "She" and "stood." Then look at how the author has elaborated by adding *where* and *how* phrases, as well as descriptive phrases about the hair. Invite students to search in their texts for other sentences that are full of description and flow. Then play the sentence-stretching game.

Start with a basic core sentence (taken or adapted from the guided-reading text), such as "My mom is from Mars" or "My friend sits across from me." Talk about adding descriptive words that tell *when, where, how, what kind,* and *why*. Work together to insert descriptive words, prepositional phrases, and even complete clauses to elaborate on the details in the sentence and make it flow smoothly.

Gift of a Word

The texts fluent readers read should include vivid vocabulary that students can use in their own writing. Have each student choose two vocabulary words from their reading that they might be able to use in their writing. They write the words on sticky notes and stick them in their writing folders, to remain there until those words have been used in their writing. When a student has used the word in a piece of writing, he or she should pass on the word to someone else to use in writing—a gift of a word.

Prompted Writing and Extended Response

Of all student groups, fluent readers are most likely to be the ones subjected to the joy of testing. Large-scale writing assessments usually take one of two forms: a general prompt (such as "tell about a time when…") or a response to reading. We owe it to our students to familiarize them with this unique writing genre so that they can get optimal credit for what they know and can do. Generally, an effective response consists of four components:

1. Umbrella statement: an overview response that uses as many words from the prompt as possible
2. Examples and details: ideas that build on and explain the response
3. Support from the text: specific evidence right from the text to support the response
4. Elaboration and insight: ideas, personal responses, or connections that go beyond what is expected

An umbrella statement is an opening statement that restates the prompt and offers a one-sentence summary of the answer. Restating the prompt in the opening sentence serves two purposes: it helps the writer clarify what the question is asking, and it indicates to the scorer that the writer has a basic understanding of what is being asked. We call it an *umbrella statement* because it covers the details that will be provided in the rest of the response.

Start by asking some simple questions from the guided-reading text and invite students to flip the questions into one-sentence responses that use as many words as possible from the prompt. This is more challenging when the prompt takes an imperative form rather than a question: for example, "Compare the characters of Goldilocks and Red Riding Hood." An umbrella statement might be "Goldilocks and Red Riding Hood are both little girls in fairy tales, but that's where the similarities end."

When students have grasped the idea of the umbrella statement, use the same approach to teach adding examples and details, offering support from the text and elaborating with insight.

Prompt: *In the story "Jack and the Beanstalk" do you think Jack was a hero or a villain?*
Umbrella Statement: *In the story "Jack and the Beanstalk" I think Jack was a villain because he was the one who committed crimes against the giant.*

Sample Fairy Tale Prompts for Practice

1. What could Little Red Riding Hood have done to prevent the problems she had?
2. What should the three bears do with Goldilocks? What would be an appropriate punishment?
3. Which of the three pigs was most important to the story? Why do you think so?
4. What would be a nonviolent way for the third billy goat to get across the bridge?
5. What is the lesson we should learn from Beauty and the Beast? Do you agree with it?
6. In Rumpelstiltskin, who is the villain and who is the hero?

(Jamison Rog, 2010)

Sample Guided Reading Lesson Plan for Fluent Readers

Title	Learning Goals
Ghost House, Chapter 1	Comprehension: Drawing inferences about characters Word Study: Interpreting slang expressions; understanding apostrophes in possessives and contractions

Text/Book Introduction

Preview:

This is a book about some boys who dare each other to spend the night in an old house that they think is haunted.

Prior Knowledge:

What would you expect to read about in a haunted house story? Make a list of the elements of a traditional "ghost story"; e.g., a ghost, strange noises, curtains moving, door slamming, thunderstorm, etc.

Purpose:

In this chapter, we meet the four main characters: Tyler, Zach, AJ, and Hammy. Remember that we learn about characters in three different ways: from what the author tells us, from what the characters themselves say and do, and from what others say about them. As you read, think about what you know about each of the characters.

Day 1	Must-Do
• Book introduction • Put Stop sign down at end of page 6. Read pages 3–6 individually • Group share: what have we learned about the characters so far? (Zach: little brother; AJ: believes in ghosts; Hammy: skateboarder; not afraid of ghosts; Tyler: not afraid; all: like to laugh, friends, hang out together) • Make a character chart with descriptions of each character and how we know • Draw attention to *inferences* that we make about characters • Have students read the rest of the chapter individually, with teacher listening in on one student at a time • After reading, add to the character chart	• Have students place Stop sign at end of chapter two. Color-code sticky notes for Zach, Hammy, and Tyler. Use 2–3 sticky notes per character and tab points of information.
Day 2	**Must-Do**
• Revisit must-do; add descriptions to character chart • Continue reading/discussing next chapter individually with pause points at pages 13, 15, 18, 20; tab more character info • Discuss slang expressions, such as *shooting off my mouth, goofing around, chipping in*	• Construct a foldable Venn diagram to compare any two of the characters. • Buddy Reading: revisit previous chapters for fluency and expression
Day 3	**Must-Do**
• Revisit must-do; group share • Word hunt: words with apostrophes. Review contractions and possessives; word sort • Guided thinking: predict what each of the boys will do and why; Which elements of a ghost story have appeared? What is author's purpose? How well has it been achieved?	Extended Response: *As Tyler, write a note to your mother, explaining where you will be all night.*

Inference Chart

What we read…	What we know…	What we infer…

Synthesizing Chart

At first we thought…	Then we read…	Now we think…

Summarizing Framework for Narrative Text

This story is about

_____

First

_____

_____

Then

_____

_____

Finally

_____

_____

At the end

_____

Pembroke Publishers ©2012 *Guiding Readers* by Lori Jamison Rog ISBN 978-1-55138-273-9

Active Bookmarks

A word on this page that some readers might have trouble with is _____.

A good way to help remember it is _____.

The character _____ reminds me of _____

because _____.

If I were the character _____, I would have _____

because_____.

The section of the book was believable/not believable because _____

_____.

Something I connected with in this part of the book was_____

because_____.

A picture I got in my mind from this section was_____.

(Describe and sketch)

This part of the book, where _____,

makes me wonder _____.

When I read _____,

I inferred that _____.

3-H Questions Chart

I wonder…	I wonder…	I wonder…	I wonder…
I think/I know…	I think/I know…	I think/I know…	I think/I know…

Techniques Writers Use

Notice It	Name it	Try it

Pembroke Publishers ©2012 *Guiding Readers* by Lori Jamison Rog ISBN 978-1-55138-273-9

7

Guiding Struggling Readers in Upper Grades

It's 15 minutes into independent-reading time in Charlie's Grade 5 classroom, but Charlie has yet to open a book. He has spent the entire time at the bookshelf, ostensibly selecting a book, but actually making funny faces at anyone who will look at him.

Like three out of every four children with reading difficulties, Charlie is a boy. He started school with limited experiences with print, struggled through activities with letters and sounds, and was usually off-task during reading time. By Grade 3, when most of his classmates were fairly fluent, Charlie was still guessing at words, relying on pictures, and avoiding books whenever he could. Now, in Grade 5, where the books are longer and the illustrations gone, Charlie is in obvious trouble.

It is often said that in primary grades we learn to read and in upper grades we read to learn. A catchy phrase, if only it were true. In reality, we never stop learning to read. Even if a reader has developed a repertoire of strategies for certain texts at manageable reading levels, there's always the unfamiliar text form, the unique language structure, the deeper theme—all presenting new reading challenges.

Most readers in Grade 4 and beyond have enough competence and confidence to tackle texts with some degree of difficulty. But that doesn't mean they no longer need guided reading. Even with skilled readers, there remains a place for small-group reading instruction as an opportunity to scaffold students as they extend their reading reach. We might pull groups together to work on a unique text form, such as website reading. We might gather students to apply familiar strategies to more sophisticated texts or build deeper layers of inference. We might work with groups to enrich the quality of their written responses to reading. These small-group opportunities enable us to support and stretch even our best readers.

Not only do small-group structures enable us to make the most of instructional time, they make assessment easier. It's much easier to judge each student's understanding, application, or metacognitive awareness when we're observing a group of four to eight students than with a whole class.

As well, guided reading can play an important role in both Tiers 1 and 2 of the Response to Intervention model (see box on page 117). This model advocates differentiated classroom instruction at its core, with layers of increasingly intensive intervention for those who struggle. The report *Academic Literacy for Adolescents* (2007) stresses that small-group interactions and active discussion of content and strategies are not merely important, but critical for underachieving readers.

> **Response to Intervention** (RTI) is a multi-tiered approach for supporting *all* students in their reading progress. It is generally described as three tiers, though there may be more layers of intervention.
> Tier 1: At its foundation is strong, differentiated classroom instruction.
> Tier 2: For students who don't thrive on the classroom instruction (generally no more than 15% of the population), short-term small-group instruction, targeted at the learners' specific needs, is implemented.
> Tier 3: A very small percentage of students (3–5%) will require intensive, individual intervention, usually sustained for a longer period of time.

In *Reading Next* (Biancarosa & Snow, 2006), recommendations for adolescent literacy instruction include scaffolded instruction in which teachers provide high support for students practicing new skills, and then gently withdraw support as students gain independence. Guided reading is one structure for providing that important gradual release of responsibility.

Small-group reading structures and policies for students in Grade 4 and beyond vary in different jurisdictions. Some districts implement regularly scheduled guided reading throughout the grades, right through to middle and high school. Others have replaced guided reading with other grouping structures, such as literature circles or reading workshop (see chapter 6). I believe there is an important place for guided reading in upper grades, along with a range of other grouping structures. For students reading at grade level or beyond, occasional small-group lessons or sequences of lessons might be appropriate for supporting them in coping with a new text form, a higher-level strategy, or a more-challenging text. For students who are struggling, regular guided reading sessions should be a part of both the classroom and the intervention process.

What Do We Know about Struggling Readers?

Obviously, there is no single mold from which all struggling readers are cast. Some students struggle with reading because of deficits in vocabulary and background knowledge. Some students are just learning to speak the language of the classroom. Some can read the words, but not infer between or beyond the lines. Some students have succumbed to the cycle of failure and have just given up on reading. Others have identified cognitive, physical, psychological, and emotional issues that can interfere with learning in general and reading in particular.

Let's face it, we're *all* struggling readers at some time or another. I'm a struggling reader when I try to make sense of the Italian newspaper or a technical manual full of unfamiliar terms. But I have many strategies up my sleeve, the motivation to tackle tough text, and the confidence to know that I will be able to grasp most of the material if I put my mind to it. That's because I'm an *independent* reader, even when I'm struggling. *Dependent* readers, on the other hand, assume that reading always comes easily—even magically—to others; they don't realize that everyone has to do some reading work sometimes. The chart below depicts some of the common differences between dependent and independent readers.

Independent Readers usually...	Dependent Readers often...
• know that some reading is harder than other reading, and have confidence that they will be able to negotiate even a tough text and keep trying, even when the going gets tough	• are dealing with long term failure as readers and often give up before they even try • assume that "good readers" never have problems with comprehension
• have a repertoire of strategies for making sense of text, and an awareness of deliberately and purposefully using those strategies	• have limited access to comprehension strategies and often give up when reading doesn't make sense
• read fluently and at an appropriate pace to maintain comprehension, slowing down and speeding up as appropriate	• read word by word, which interferes with overall comprehension
• have a strong vocabulary and background-knowledge base from which to draw when making connections during reading	• lack an adequate vocabulary and knowledge base or fail to draw on the knowledge they have to aid in comprehension
• know when something doesn't make sense and draw on a range of strategies to fix their comprehension	• often don't even know when they don't understand and simply read on
• choose to read, and read a lot, further building their background knowledge and reading skill	• avoid reading as much as possible, and might behave inappropriately during reading time

Although every struggling reader is unique, there are a few characteristics that have in common. For one thing, they tend not to monitor their own comprehension effectively. Independent readers hit clunks (see page 99) in comprehension all the time—but they know when they don't get it and have a repertoire of strategies to fix up the mix-ups; dependent readers often don't even realize that they don't understand what they're reading, and plow right on, compounding their confusion. Or they might identify where their difficulty occurs and just stop reading, with neither the skill nor the will to correct the misunderstandings. As well, struggling readers don't choose to read and, in fact, will often avoid it at all costs. But the research on reading volume is clear: the more you read, the better you read. Not only that, the more you read, the more you know about the world around you. For many of our struggling readers, a lack of background knowledge (especially vocabulary) is one of the biggest impediments to reading comprehension. Finally, I have never met a reader—dependent or independent—who isn't fully aware of the importance of being an effective reader. They might pretend otherwise, but deep down, *every* reader wants to be a *good* reader.

> **The Research on Reading Volume with Grade 5 Students**
>
> • Students scoring at the 90th percentile on standardized tests read an average of 40 minutes a day, for a total of over 2 million words a year.
> • Students scoring at the 50th percentile read an average of 13 minutes a day, for a total of 600,000 words a year.
> • Students scoring at the 10th percentile read an average of less than 2 minutes per day, for a total of 50,000 words a year.
>
> (Anderson, Wilson & Fielding, 1988)

It's estimated that only about 10% of struggling adolescent readers need work on decoding.

In the past, we've assumed that readers who struggled simply needed more drill on skills. So while our struggling readers pored over worksheets on decoding, our independent readers read books. And what happened? The students who needed reading the most got the fewest opportunities to read. In other words, the rich got richer and the poor got poorer. Yet most adolescents reading below grade level actually can read the words on the page with reasonable accuracy and fluency. It is generally estimated that only about 10% of striving readers need intervention in decoding skills (Snow & Biancarosa, 2006). In most cases, they can read the words; the problem is that they don't always understand the ideas behind the words.

There are many different reasons why readers don't comprehend what they read. That's why it's important to thoroughly assess the needs of striving readers in order to provide instruction to meet those unique needs.

And what should that instruction look like? The report *Academic Literacy Instruction for Adolescents* states that "the content of effective literacy instruction for students reading below grade is very similar to that recommended for students reading at grade level and above." In other words, struggling readers need the same good teaching that all readers need. But they need it even more. (Torgeson et al. 2007: 89)

The strategies described in previous chapters, particularly those for developing and fluent readers, can all be adapted for struggling readers in upper grades, using text appropriate to their reading levels. As well, in this chapter we will look at three keys for supporting struggling readers: choosing appropriate texts; using assessment to guide instruction; and implementing teaching routines to reinforce reading skills and strategies.

Choosing Appropriate Texts

Perhaps the most important role teachers can play in supporting readers is to provide them with reading materials that match their abilities and their interests. Most struggling readers have already spent too much time with books that are simply too hard. Research tells us that it is not only ineffective, but also *damaging* for struggling readers to be continually confronted with texts that are too difficult for them (Allington, 2006). In fact, when selecting texts for struggling readers (and, perhaps, all readers), it is better to err on the side of too-easy than too-hard. Remember that these students have often experienced several years of school reading failure—and, with it, loss of confidence in themselves as readers. This can take a toll, not just on their reading growth, but also on their willingness to even try.

Readability Formulas

At upper-elementary years and beyond, leveling systems have limited usefulness for making the reader–text match. Many of the criteria that distinguish one level from another—illustrative support, predictability, print size and placement—just don't apply to upper-level texts. That's where the science of readability comes in. The traditional tools for measuring the degree of challenge in a text are mathematical readability formulas. There are many different formulas—Fry, Flesch-Kincaid, and Dale-Chall, to name a few—that assign a readability score, described as a grade-level equivalent, generally based on the length of the words and the length of the sentences. Most formulas have no way of judging the difficulty of a particular word for a particular reader, so they use syllable count to determine the average word length, on the assumption that longer words are more difficult to read. The Lexile system uses similar criteria, as well as a

"There is little evidence that children experiencing difficulties learning to read, even those with identifiable learning disabilities, need radically different sorts of supports than children at low risk, although they may need much more intensive support. Excellent instruction is the best intervention for children who demonstrate problems learning to read." (Snow et al., 1998: 3)

Instructional-level texts for struggling readers should present no more than 3–5% challenging words and concepts. Books for independent reading should contain no words or concepts to challenge the reader.

There is little discernable difference between a passage leveled at grade 3.5 and one at grade 3.7. It is more useful for classroom instruction to think of materials as "mid-Grade 3" or "beginning-Grade 5."

Your computer will measure the readability of a passage for you! In Word, go to Options, and in the section where you can ask for spelling or grammar check, check the box beside *Show readability statistics*.

Another technological tool is the Juicy Studio website, which provides information on readability tests for print and websites: juicystudio.com/services/readability.php#readweb

Readability statistics can tell us only what challenges the book brings to the reading experiences. It takes a wise teacher, with good knowledge of his/her students, to factor the reader into the equation.

measure of the percentage of familiar or unique words in a text. It provides a numeric score between 200 and 2000, which also correlates in a general way to grade-level reading.

We all know that there are numerous limitations to these formulas. Many multisyllabic words, such as *transportation*, *computer*, and *electricity*, are common and quite decodable. On the other hand, if you toss the name of my home town of Saskatoon, Saskatchewan, into a 100-word passage, the readability shoots through the roof! Yet it shouldn't present any great challenge even to struggling readers who live in that city.

So how can we use this information to match readers with appropriate books for guided reading instruction? Let's say, for example, that you have conducted an oral reading record and determined that a passage at Grade 3.5 readability is appropriate instructional level (in other words, at least 95% support and no more than 5% challenge) for a particular grade 6 student. However, that doesn't mean that just any passage at mid–Grade-3 reading level will be appropriate for that student. We need to use our professional judgment to determine whether it is really the right book for that reader. For example, we need to ask ourselves

- How many challenging words is this reader likely to struggle with? (For example, are the words *Saskatoon, Saskatchewan* likely to be a breeze or a bugaboo?)
- What is the concept load of this passage? Is the reader likely to have the necessary background knowledge to understand the material?
- Are the text structure and features likely to add an additional challenge for this reader? For example, are there charts and tables, maps, or other text features that might be unfamiliar? Are there flashbacks, foreshadowing, or other literary elements that could be confusing to a literal reader?
- Is the reader likely to be interested in the topic and motivated to read this material? (Boys, for example, are largely unwilling to get anywhere near a text if it has a girl as the main character.)

Fortunately, there is much to choose from in the world of children's and young-adult print literature, the Internet, and the many forms of functional text in the world around us. As long as we understand a bit about the art and science of readability, the features of a text that make it more or less challenging, and the needs and interests of our students, we will be able to make that sensitive reader–text match.

"Leveled" little books have even been published for adolescent students. However, no one is more sensitive about the "baby book" than our struggling readers! If it's too thin to have a spine, they probably will be reluctant to read it, even in the safety of the guided reading lesson, much less in the more-public setting of independent reading. However, resources like magazine articles, texts printed from (or read on) the computer, or directions on how to program your PVR can be adapted for any reader.

Novels and chapter books have the advantage of looking like the books that all the other kids are reading. However, their technical readability is likely to rise and fall several times throughout the book. Some publishers will print a grade level on the back of a book (the kiss of death for a struggling reader). However, this usually means that they've taken an average of all the words and sentences in an entire book. Katherine Patterson's *Bridge to Terabithia*, for example, is frequently used in Grade 5 classrooms. The Flesch-Kincaid grade level readability is 4.4—sounds pretty manageable but, in truth, it likely means that there are some sections as easy as Grade 2 readability and some that might be as high as Grade 8. Of course, we never read an entire novel in guided-reading groups. But if we decide that reading *Bridge to Terabithia* is important for a below–grade-level guided-reading group, then we need to find an excerpt that is within the reading range of those students.

Hi-Lo Texts

Most novels and other trade books were written to provide interesting content and literary quality, not supports for struggling readers. *Hi-lo* books are designed to offer readers high interest and low vocabulary (or difficulty).

Some materials are written specifically to be engaging but easy to read. At best, these hi-lo books contain interesting stories (or information), written in an appealing style, with controls on vocabulary and other text features to support struggling readers. Unfortunately, as with any other product, some books are better than others. There are many books professing to be hi-lo that are neither interesting to kids nor easy to read.

When looking for high-interest/low-vocabulary reading materials for struggling readers, probably the two most important considerations are content and appearance. The stories and nonfiction should be on themes of interest to the age of students; just because a fifth grader is reading at Grade 2 level doesn't mean that he wants to read the same things that seven-year-olds read. And we want to find books that don't look different from the books that other students are reading. This is where the Goldilocks principle comes in: the book has to be long enough to look like a regular novel, but not so long as to intimidate striving readers. Publishers have different tricks for padding out an otherwise short novel: occasional illustrations, starting each chapter halfway down the page, slightly enlarged spaces between lines. However, be careful to avoid books with oversized print and unusual fonts: large print might appeal to those of us beginning to suffer from presbyopia, but it might as well flash "*special*" in neon lights in the eyes of adolescents.

Some other considerations in choosing good hi-lo books include

- consistent readability throughout the book; no peaks and valleys in degree of difficulty
- appealing covers that grab attention
- action in the first few pages of text; cliffhanger chapter endings that motivate readers to keep reading
- age-appropriate illustrations that make the book longer without making it harder, and provide visual support for understanding the text
- characters that are older than the readers
- limited numbers of challenging or unique words
- few or no literary devices and figurative language

Author Paul Kropp reminds us to BEAR these things in mind when choosing fiction for boys:
- **B**oys (or men) as main characters
- **E**pisodic (a series of events rather than a long drawn-out plot line)
- **A**ction-oriented (rather than introspective or descriptive)
- **R**ebellious (focus on the outsider, the misdeed, the event that pushes the boundaries of social conventions)

A discussion of struggling readers would be incomplete without some mention of the unique challenges of finding books for boys. Most boys won't touch a book with a girl as the main character. Boys tend to prefer action (preferably with some degree of violence) to literary language and character development. But the reality is that the majority of our struggling readers are boys and we need to make that extra effort to find books that our boys can and want to read.

Using Assessment to Guide Instruction

So we know the relative difficulty of a particular text. How does this help us match that text to a group of readers? The best assessment is an individual oral reading record. Many teachers take an oral reading record "on the run" (hence the term "running record"), but there are also many published assessments with graded reading passages. Testing with grade-level reading materials might be necessary for report cards or large-scale assessments, but we rarely need a formal test to tell us which students are not coping with grade-level materials. Furthermore, this information is not particularly useful in planning instruction. We already know what kind of text is *not* appropriate; we need to know what types of texts *are* appropriate.

Here's a simple oral reading record process: Choose a 100-word passage that you have estimated to be at appropriate reading level. Sit beside the student as he/she reads the passage out loud, and keep track of the errors, or miscues, that the reader makes. If the student has made 3–5 mistakes in 100 words, conduct a quick comprehension check—either a retelling or response to a few questions. If the student demonstrates adequate general, but not insightful, comprehension, then this is likely an appropriate instructional-level text for the student. Use this text as a benchmark to select other texts for guided reading. If the student makes only one or two errors—or none at all—and demonstrates thorough comprehension, this text is at that student's independent reading level. This is useful information for helping that student choose texts for free-choice reading. Try the oral reading check again with a slightly more challenging text. If the student makes six or more miscues, then the text is simply too hard. Don't even bother with a comprehension check. Choose a less-challenging text and try another oral reading assessment. Keep trying till you find the right level.

The great thing about an oral reading record is that it provides us with much more information than the reader–text match. We can hear whether the student is reading at an appropriate pace, with expression and fluency. We can determine whether the reader is comprehending at a superficial or deeper level. We can analyze what types of miscues the reader is making: Is he/she over-relying on sounding out? Does he/she self-correct, or keep on reading even when the errors interfere with the meaning of the passage?

The time taken to conduct a brief oral reading record with every student at least once per reporting period—more frequently with our struggling readers—is well worth it.

Lesson Routines

I said it before and I'll say it again: Our struggling readers need the same good teaching that our capable readers need—but they need it even more. The principles and elements of good guided reading instruction outlined earlier in the book are even more important for reluctant readers:

- texts that offer at least 95% support and no more than 5% challenge
- many opportunities for connected reading
- plenty of talk about text and reading processes to develop metacognition
- explicit teaching, guided support, and independent practice of strategies and skills

The term *miscue* refers to words that the reader has omitted, inserted, or substituted for words that are actually in the text. These are clues that the reader is not using his or her cueing systems effectively. Keeping track of the miscues readers make helps us plan instruction that meets their needs.

Most independent readers don't need external incentives to read. The reading is the reward in itself. But many dependent readers have already experienced enough failure to perceive that reading is a punishment to be avoided at all costs. We might never convince them that reading is fun, but we can offer engaging and interesting experiences that teach them that reading is something they will be able to do. That's why so many of the teaching routines in this chapter involve jokes and riddles, games and movement. We use sticky notes and bookmarks rather than journals, foldables instead of graphic organizers, active games instead of seatwork.

Our guided reading instruction should focus on helping students build strategic independence, not just helping them tackle today's text.

There are many ways that, as teachers, we can mitigate the challenge of tough texts. Preteaching vocabulary, building background knowledge with anticipation guides, and providing study guides or outlines to follow are some of the techniques we use to support students in content-area reading. But these routines help with understanding only one particular text. Our job is to provide struggling readers with the competence and confidence to read when we're not around to support them.

See page 130 for a sample lesson plan for guided reading for struggling readers.

We're not doing our students any favors with band-aids like "week-ahead reading," where a learning-support teacher simply reads the whole-class passage to a student ahead of time so that student can "read" it with the rest of the class. We've got to rethink the prevalence of whole-class instruction with one common text. One size doesn't fit all in tennis shoes or T-shirts; why would we presume that one size would fit all in learning? Struggling readers are already functioning behind their age-level peers; their growth needs to be accelerated if they are to catch up. The following routines for comprehension, word-solving, fluency, and reader response are appropriate for any readers, but they have been teacher-tested and pupil-proven to work with many struggling readers.

Comprehension Strategies

The guided-reading structure provides opportunities for both individual strategies and flexible use of a range of strategies. In reality, we never use just a single strategy during reading. But independent readers have a repertoire of strategies on which to draw. Sometimes struggling readers need to master a single strategy at a time to stock their comprehension toolbox.

Many sticky-note comprehension strategies are discussed in chapters 5 and 6. They are every bit as appropriate for struggling readers as for independent readers. Here are some additional comprehension routines.

Comic Strip Inferences

Learning Goal: Students will be able to identify inferences required to understand humor.

You have to infer in order to understand what you read. All of us, even our struggling readers, are always drawing inferences. So the first step is to make our students metacognitive about what they do when they infer. Readers infer by combining the information that we read with what we already know from our background knowledge to come up with an understanding that is implied, but not explicitly stated, in the text.

See The Inference Equation on page 98.

> **Sample of the Inference Equation**
>
> What I Read: "When I woke up in the morning, there were leaves and branches all over the yard."
> What I Know: Storms cause leaves and branches to blow off trees.
> What I Infer: There was a big storm overnight.

One of the most engaging routines to help any readers think about what they do when they infer is reading cartoons. Appreciating humor always requires inference. In most cases, we're amused by what is *not* directly stated, but what we fill in from our background knowledge. Take, for example, a silly joke: "What do prehistoric creatures do when they sleep? Dinosnore." In order to appreciate the fine level of humor, you have to combine what you just read with the background knowledge that prehistoric creatures are called dinosaurs and many people snore when they sleep. *What I read* plus *what I know* equals *what I infer*.

Cartoons add a visual element to the process, making it easier and more fun to read. Your local newspaper can be a source of many age- and family-appropriate comic strips. Keep a file of cartoons for practicing the inference process.

Display a copy of some easy jokes or cartoons. Make a two-column chart on a piece of paper: in one column, note all the things you observe in the illustration and the text. In the second column, indicate the background knowledge necessary to "get" the joke. For example, here's what we observed from the illustrations and text of a cartoon from the newspaper: A dentist is standing in front of a display stand full of marbles with a sign that says, "*Bite down on a marble, 25 cents*"; the caption reads, *When Dentists Drum Up Business*. In order to appreciate the humor, we need to know the following: what happens to your teeth when you bite a marble; what kind of work a dentist does; and what it means to "drum up business."

Must-Do

Provide students with individual copies of jokes or riddles and have them work with a partner (or independently) to complete a two-column chart like the one created in the lesson.

Remote-Control Reading

Learning Goal: Students will be able to pause in reading to monitor their own comprehension.

One of the biggest challenges for struggling readers is monitoring their own comprehension. Too often, our striving readers don't even realize that they don't understand what they're reading and plod painfully on, compounding their confusion. Other times, they know they don't get it, but don't know when they stopped getting it. Sometimes, they simply stop reading and give up.

On page 98, we described Clicks and Clunks, a self-monitoring routine in which readers practice tabbing points of confusion with red flags, then replacing the red flags with green flags when they are able to correct the confusion.

Another way to teach students about self-monitoring while reading is to compare it to using a remote control to watch TV or a movie. Just as we press the Play button to start our show, we press the Play button in our brains to start reading. However, every now and then (let's say, every page), we need to hit the Pause button in our brains and ask ourselves, "Is this making sense to me? Do I understand all of this? What did I just read?" If we answer ourselves, "Yes, this makes sense!" then we hit that mental Play button again and keep on reading. But if our answer is no, then we need to hit the Stop button and hit either Rewind or Fast Forward to use our strategies to fix up the mix-up.

Some teachers provide each student with a bookmark, labeled with the symbols in the box in the margin. But it's easy to find inexpensive remote-control devices at a dollar store and add the labels to the back. That way, fidgeters can actually feel like they are physically hitting the buttons as they use the "clickers" in their brains.

Must-Do

Provide each student with their own controller and a passage to read on their own using remote-control reading to monitor their comprehension.

Chunk the Sentence

As we have seen in readability research, sentence length has a big impact on the degree of challenge a passage presents for readers. This is particularly true for our dysfluent word-by-word readers, who often have trouble remembering the beginning of a sentence long enough to get to the end. We can teach readers to negotiate convoluted sentences by chunking those sentences into clauses and phrases, using punctuation marks and signal words. Here are some signals we can teach students:

- **Colons and Semicolons** are the most obvious signals, as they generally attach two related sentences to one another.
- **Commas** often separate clauses and phrases (with the exception of commas that separate words in a list).
- **Conjunctions**, both coordinate (*and, but, or, so*) and subordinate (*when, because, although, if*), indicate the separation of clauses in a sentence.
- **Prepositions** start phrases that usually indicate time or place, such as *after, in, to, over, without*.

Take this example from Paul Kropp's novel *One Crazy Night*:

Back in Grade Five, I was rinsing some paint brushes in the sink when the fire alarm went off. I told Mrs. P. that I couldn't turn the faucet off, but she ignored me, so I just lined up with the other kids and we all marched outside in single file.

That second sentence is 32 words long! But looking at the conjunctions, we can chunk the very long sentence into four short sentences:

I told Mrs. P that I couldn't turn the faucet off. She ignored me. I just lined up with the other kids. We all marched outside in single file.

Technically, we might even consider "that I couldn't turn the faucet off" another clause, but this might make the text more, rather than less, confusing.

Gather sentences from the guided reading passage—or, better yet, send students into the text to find sentences that they consider formidable. As a group, practice chunking these sentences into phrases and clauses. You might find it helpful to write the sentences on sentence strips and have the students physically cut them apart to break them into chunks. Then go back into the sentence and practice reading it with fluency and phrasing, attending to punctuation and meaning.

Remote Control Buttons
➤   Play
▫▫ Pause
■   Stop
◀◀ Rewind
▶▶ Fast Forward

Learning Goal: Students will be able to navigate complex sentences by breaking them into phrases and clauses.

Must-Do

Provide students with a set of sentences from the current guided-reading text or past guided-reading texts. Have them use slash marks to break each sentence into manageable chunks.

Visualizing: Story Wheels

The ability to generate mental images during and after reading is considered to be a key comprehension strategy (Pearson & Duke, 2000). For many readers, this process is automatic; reading is almost like watching a movie running through in their minds. For others (myself included, I confess), visualization is a strategy that must be activated deliberately and purposefully. Graphic organizers are excellent tools for helping students organize information that they read in a visual way.

One way to reinforce visualization during reading is to teach students to pause periodically and "Click!" with their mental cameras, thinking aloud or to themselves about the images that are generated. Start by selecting two or three pause points in the reading. When students reach those points, they stop and describe the picture in their minds. Sometimes I will have students place two or three large sticky notes in strategic places in the text they are about to read. As they come to these stickies in their reading, they are to pause and sketch the image the comes to their minds. Labeled diagrams, such as the mind map described on page 141, provide opportunities to put their images on paper.

Must-Do

Create circular foldables by folding thin paper plates into six sections. (See page 161 in the Appendix for instructions.) Fold up the point to make a hexagonal shape in the middle when it's unfolded. Write the title of the book or passage in the centre shape. In the first section, sketch and caption the beginning of the story and add a caption. In the next four sections, sketch and caption four key events. In the final section, sketch and caption the end of the story. During the next guided reading lesson, have students share and explain their circle stories to their reading partners.

Mapping the Page

Informational text often has a mixture of print and visuals on a page, and reading in a linear fashion from top to bottom and left to right virtually guarantees that some key information will be missed. Readers often miss captions or labels on pictures and even text boxes that do not follow a top-to-bottom left-to-right orientation. This routine teaches students to locate where the all the information can be found on a page.

Use a guided-reading text that has captions, labels, or other information in addition to the illustrations and print. Clip a clear acetate sheet (e.g., an overhead transparency) over the page. As students point out where the different bits of information are found, use markers to draw boxes or circles around the sections in different colors. Be sure to box every label, caption, heading, etc. When you remove the clear sheet, you have a visual map of the different places you need to read in order to get all the information on the page.

After working through the process together, give each student a piece of acetate to clip to a designated page in their books, and have them chart their own maps of information. Then, as they read the page, have them use the markers to check off each piece of information as they read it. You might even suggest that

If water-soluble markers are used, the acetate sheets can be cleaned and reused.

they number each box (or circle) as they read it, then go back and compare the order of reading with a partner. This could generate a good discussion about the difference between reading styles for fiction and nonfiction visual texts.

Most large-scale reading assessments contain some visual text. If students are permitted to mark the reading passages on large-scale assessments, this is a good strategy to ensure that they are getting all the pieces on visual texts.

Must-Do

Use another text or a different excerpt from the guided-reading text for students to go through the page-mapping process independently.

Fluency Routines

Fluent oral reading does not guarantee strong comprehension. But dysfluent reading pretty much guarantees that a reader will run into comprehension difficulties. Readers who call out every word often fail to understand a lengthy sentence, much less the overall text. Helping our struggling readers build fluency can be a key to smoothing out many reading problems.

The only way to build fluency is to practice reading aloud, and there are several ways to support fluent, expressive oral reading. Round-robin reading is not one of them. No one ever became a better reader by listening to someone struggle painfully through a text that was too hard, but plenty of people learned to hate reading even more than they already did. Never ask any reader—particularly a struggling reader—to read publicly unless he or she has a chance to practice reading the text first.

Guided repeated oral reading has been identified by the National Reading Panel (NICHD, 2000) as one of the best techniques for building fluency. This technique has several variations, but generally involves modeling the reading, then having the student reread the same passage several times, each time receiving specific feedback on how to improve the reading the next time.

Offer specific suggestions for students:

- Say each word clearly and not too quickly, as though you're talking to someone who might not understand.
- Don't stop at the end of the line unless there is punctuation.
- Pay attention to punctuation marks. They are the traffic signals of reading.
- Read in groups of words rather than word by word. Think about which words go together.
- Change the expression of your voice to match the meaning of the text, especially when there is a question mark, exclamation mark, or special print.
- Don't make your voice dip down at the end of each sentence.

Choral reading can be a great support for struggling readers, as it pulls them along in expression, tempo, and phrasing. Performance reading, such as readers theatre, provides purpose for rereading to build expression, clarity, and fluency. (See chapter 5 for ideas for readers theatre lessons.)

Must-Do

- Telling jokes is a motivating way to get students to rehearse a reading passage. Have students research and print out jokes (be sure to screen it first for class-appropriateness). They should read their jokes several times to practice when to pause and when to speed up, when to speak loudly and when to use a quiet voice, etc. in order for the joke to have the most impact.

- Provide pairs of students with a short poem that you have read together. Have them practice reading the poem to perform it for the group. They should decide which lines each will read and which they will read together, when their voices should be loud and when soft, etc.

The Reading–Writing Connection

Let's face it: just about all our struggling readers are also struggling writers. So when we assess their reading proficiency based on written responses, we're hitting them with a double-whammy. That's why so many struggling readers don't get credit on tests for what they do know. If we want accurate classroom assessments of what our students know and can do as readers, perhaps we need to make accommodations, allowing them to respond orally or to have their responses scribed. Also, maybe this is the time to overlook issues with spelling and conventions and instead focus on the content of the response.

Many students simply don't know how to respond to reading beyond "I liked it" or "It was boring." The small-group setting is an appropriate place to model and practice written responses. Kylene Beers (2003) suggests that often we need to teach students the words they need for responding to reading, both orally and in writing, such as in an anchor chart.

Words that make you sound smart when you're talking about reading:

- A realistic/unrealistic situation
- A suspenseful/predictable plot
- An authentic/unbelievable character
- A powerful/weak message
- Descriptive/mundane words
- A fast-moving/plodding storyline
- Unique/overdone descriptions
- Elaborate/sketchy ideas

Graphic organizers are particularly useful for struggling writers. For one thing, they are less intimidating than a blank piece of paper or journal page, because they limit writing space to a chart or box. As well, they help struggling readers organize their thinking by putting the information into a visual framework.

Responses that transform what was read into a different text form can support both reading comprehension and writing proficiency. For example, students might be asked to reframe elements of a story as a

- newspaper article
- how-to (procedure)
- anagram poem (e.g., using the letters in a character's name)
- letter or diary to/from a character
- Craigslist or E-bay ad
- character's Facebook page

Asking struggling readers to write in response to reading might seem like adding insult to injury. But according to Michael McKenna,

> By asking students to use the information they find in sentences and paragraphs to complete charts, build diagrams, write summaries or engage in similar tasks, they must process and understand what they read. (McKenna, 2002: 8)

Small-group guided writing instruction not only supports struggling learners in transferring their ideas to paper, it also helps them become more competent readers.

Sample Guided Reading Lesson Plan for Struggling Readers

Title	Learning Goals
Choose Your Bully, chapters 3-4	Comprehension: Drawing inferences from text Word Study: similes Vocabulary: research, solution, various, target Fluency: Readers Theatre script of Ch 3-4

Text/Book Introduction

Preview:

This is a book about two kids, Ling and Richard, who are being bullied by a guy named Chuck. They need to do some research to find a solution to their problem. Read p. 18 together to establish context; think aloud, modeling inferences; e.g., I'm inferring that Chuck pushed Ling to the ground and the ground is wet because she said the back of her pants were wet and she is embarrassed.

Prior Knowledge:

TTYN – What's the best thing to do if you're being bullied?

Purpose:

Today as we read, we're going to talk to our brains about what we know in our background knowledge that helps us understand this text.

Day 1	Must-Do
• Book Introduction: read p. 18 aloud while students follow in their texts • Pause Point: end of p. 19 – any inferences? Prompt with questioning if necessary: *Did Ling beat Chuck up? How do you know? Why did Ling say, "aggh!" Why was Chuck eating Richard's lunch?* • Introduce "how to" list on p. 20. Pause point on p. 20. Predict which solution they will pick. TTYN: Which solution would you choose and why? • Continue reading as time permits	• Read all of chapter 3 independently • Complete a graphic organizer—They Think/I Think (independently or in pairs)
Day 2 • Share must-do/reread text in pairs • Summarize: main idea, key points • Predict: How do you think their solution will work? • Review vocabulary • Word study: find examples of similes (Note sarcasm in "nice as a pit bull")	**Must-Do** • Create a picture glossary for two of the similes in the text • Read next two chapters in text independently
Day 3 • Share must-do • Introduce readers theatre: script format, roles, etc. • First read, sharing roles	**Must-Do** Practice readers theatre to perform at next GR session

8

The Nonfiction Connection

Jackson (our fluent reader from chapter 6) was a bit of a late bloomer when it came to reading. He was much more interested in Lego than in letters in Kindergarten, acted out during DEAR time in Grade 1, and avoided reading as much as possible in Grade 2. But suddenly, in Grade 3, he discovered the Guinness Book of World Records and he had an epiphany. The fascinating facts and strange events drew him into the book over and over, and hardly a day went by without Jackson regaling the other students with the latest amazing record.

There are many students like Jackson who are engaged by nonfiction in a way that fiction can't match. Yet access to nonfiction text has traditionally been limited in elementary classrooms, particularly in the primary grades. In her classic 2000 study, Nell Duke reported that first graders in the U.S. experienced, on average, less than three minutes of exposure to informational texts each day!

Increasing awareness of the importance of informational reading has created a rising demand for nonfiction texts at early reading levels. As well, informational texts for young readers have become richer and more interesting, with wonderful photographic illustrations and other text features. The guided reading lesson is the perfect forum for students to practice reading informational material—or info-text—at their instructional-reading levels, in small groups with teacher support.

Challenges and Supports in Info-Text

Reading nonfiction requires all the comprehension that reading fiction demands: connecting, questioning, inferring, monitoring and clarifying, synthesizing, and so on. But there are unique challenges to nonfiction as well:

- Nonfiction tends to be more "dense" with information than fiction. Conventional wisdom suggests that a reader can skip at least one in 15 words in a fiction text and still comprehend the passage. It's not so simple with nonfiction text. Missing one key term or fact may very well interfere with understanding a big part of the text.
- Although good nonfiction today is written with as much voice as a narrative text, there is a different tone to nonfiction that might be unfamiliar to young readers more accustomed to stories.

- Nonfiction often conveys information using a range of print and visual modes: text, illustrations, graphs and tables, and other visuals. Sometimes there are many different visuals in different places on one page.
- Nonfiction is not read in a linear fashion—top to bottom, left to right—as fiction is. Readers bounce around in nonfiction, homing in on portions of interest, jumping from text to visuals, and even skipping sections of text that might not suit their interest or purposes.

Although nonfiction lacks the familiar structures of narrative text, it offers many other supports to readers. The problem is, too many readers aren't aware of these supports or aren't metacognitive about how they can help. Take a look at some of the features of nonfiction text that aid readers:

- Nonfiction is often broken down into chunks of text on a subtopic, which helps the reader process smaller amounts of information at a time. It also adds white space, making the page look more reader-friendly.
- Headings and subheadings organize information for readers and let them know what is coming next.
- Topic sentences often encapsulate the main ideas in a paragraph and enable the reader to predict information that might be encountered in subsequent sentences.
- Vocabulary supports are more common than in fiction; these include context clues and even definitions and pronunciation keys.
- Illustrations and other visuals provide nontextual information and add interest to the page.
- Organizers, such as tables of contents, glossaries, and indexes, help readers locate specific information.
- Bold or colored print or unique fonts help draw readers' attention to important words or ideas.

Matching Readers and Texts

We've all taught students who can read a narrative text with ease, but fall apart when confronted with a nonfiction text at the same level. Some of the reasons are described in the preceding section. At emergent levels, pretty much all texts are nonfiction: "This is a…" or "I put on my…" are typical texts—simply captions describing a picture. But by the time readers reach developing and fluent levels, distinctions between narrative and informational texts are wider and there is a greater range of nonfiction text forms and structures.

Nonfiction texts for young readers should be current, accurate, and objective.

What should we look for in good nonfiction texts for guided reading? As with any nonfiction text selection, look for material that is current, authentic, and carefully written to support readers at the appropriate level of instruction. Take care to avoid stereotyping and author bias, unless you have a specific reason to draw students' attention to these features for critical reading. Try to find topics of particular interest to your students. Look for text supports, such as those described above.

There are many excellent collections of leveled nonfiction books available, even for the youngest readers. But leveled books are not the only sources of informational texts for guided reading. Magazine articles, nonfiction trade books, and educational websites are excellent sources of print and online reading. If the material has not been externally leveled, you'll have to draw on your own

Remember the 95% success/5% challenge maxim. We want the students to be able to read most of the text on their own, but encounter just enough challenge to require them to draw on their strategies and do some reading work.

knowledge of text supports and challenges to estimate the level of difficulty and the appropriateness of the text for a particular group.

If your students are in Grade 3 and beyond, a technical readability assessment can provide a rough estimate of the difficulty level of a passage. (For more information on readability, see chapter 7.) One indication of the degree of challenge of a text is the quantity and placement of print on the page and the amount of illustrative support. However, in some nonfiction texts, there are so many visuals that they can become more of a distraction than a support. Take a closer look at the text. Are there lengthy complex sentences and a lot of challenging vocabulary? What about the concept load? Will the students have the background knowledge necessary to access this material with just a bit of challenge?

In addition to the reading level, you'll want to look for texts that meet particular instructional purposes. Do you want your students to work with text features such as bold print or subtitles? Do you want them to practice using context clues to solve unfamiliar words? As with fiction reading, the text must address both the level of difficulty and the lesson focus.

The Guided Reading Lesson with Informational Texts

The format of the guided reading lesson sequence with nonfiction text doesn't look much different from the format using fiction text: set learning goals, choose appropriate texts, introduce the text, guide and scaffold as students read, follow up with rereading and extended experience with the text.

Choosing nonfiction texts for guided reading can be a little more difficult than it is with fiction, because much of the challenge for a reader is contingent on the students' familiarity and background knowledge of the topic. However, a careful book introduction can mitigate some of the challenges. Sometimes preteaching a few key vocabulary words can make a difficult text more accessible. However, we need to keep our lesson goals in mind: Is the purpose of the lesson to help students read this particular text or to develop a set of strategies to read beyond this text? We won't always be available to provide students with vocabulary instruction or an advance organizer; these are merely scaffolds on the journey to independence.

Before-Reading Routines

Four Ps Book Introduction
1. **P**review the text
2. Activate **P**rior knowledge
3. **P**reteach key vocabulary or concepts
4. Set a **P**urpose for reading

Earlier in the text, we discussed the three Ps of prereading: preview the text, activate prior knowledge, and set a purpose for reading. Of these, activating background knowledge is probably the most important challenge in preparing students to read a nonfiction text. Writers of nonfiction often assume that readers have a certain amount of background knowledge on the topic. Readers who struggle might not have the requisite background knowledge, or might not know how to access the background knowledge they have. It may be necessary to add another P—Preteaching—to introduce critical vocabulary or essential concepts.

More than 30 years ago, Donna Ogle gave us the gift of the K-W-L Organizer (What I Know, What I Want to find out, What I Learned). Since that time, educators have been adapting and modifying it to suit their own instructional purposes. My favorite adaptation is Tony Stead's RAN (Reading and Analyzing Nonfiction) Chart (Stead, 2006), which I've modified into What We Think We Know.

What We Think We Know

Learning Goal: Students will be able to activate prior knowledge before reading, then generate information acquired from reading informational text.

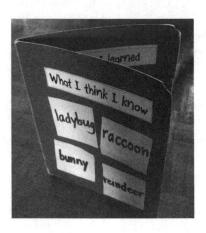

I create a What We Think We Know chart by folding a piece of chart paper in half to form a booklet or using a file folder (see sample in margin). On the outside, write *What We Think We Know*; on the two inside pages, write *We Were Right!* and *What We Learned*. The back page says, *What We Wonder*. Framing the information as "what we *think* we know" frees up readers to speculate or take some guesses, at least to open their minds to the topic.

Together, we generate ideas about what students think they know about the topic of the reading. I generally accept any reasonable suggestion (and what is considered "reasonable" might look quite different in Kindergarten than in Grade 3) and write each idea on a sticky note to attach to the front of the chart. These ideas will help set a purpose for reading, as students read to see which of their facts are confirmed in the reading. After reading, we revisit the facts on the front of the chart to see which are validated in the text. These sticky notes are moved from the front of the chart to the inside. (Using the booklet format in this way, the unconfirmed facts remain out of sight.) Then we use the What We Learned page to add new facts. Now we have a chart full of information acquired from the reading.

The What We Wonder heading on the back can be used before reading, after reading, or both. Sometimes readers don't know what they wonder until they've done some reading on the topic; sometimes the reading generates new questions. The wonderings help focus the reading and inspire further reading.

Must-Do

- Have students fold a piece of paper in four and note in each section one thing they already knew (that was confirmed), two things they learned, and one thing they wonder. This might take the form of labeled pictures for younger students or struggling readers.
- Higher-level readers might use their own What We Think We Know charts, made from 8" x 11" file folders. After completing a few of these together, have students complete their own charts before, during, and after reading.

Get HIP to Reading

Learning Goal: Students will be able to preview texts before reading by scanning headings, pictures, and the introduction.

Taking a quick preview of the text before reading is one of the habits of highly effective readers. Previewing the text helps readers get the gist of what the passage is about, activates background knowledge, and establishes a context for the reading. Getting hip (or in the know) is getting ready to read! Teach students that, before they embark on a nonfiction reading task, they should take a quick preview of three things:

- **H**eadings give an indication of important topics that will be covered.
- **I**ntroductions provide an overview of what the text will be about.
- **P**ictures offer snapshots of some key ideas.

The acronym HIP reminds readers to look at three things before reading:
- **H**eadings
- **I**ntroduction
- **P**ictures

Using an informational text that contains these three text features, first read the introduction together and have students talk to a reading partner about what they know so far about the text, what they predict will be included, and what they wonder. Repeat the process by reading through the headings or subtitles in the chapter or short section of text, and then talking about the pictures. Tell students that the things they have discussed with a partner will be the things that they think about when they read on their own.

Before assigning the must-do, be sure to practice talking through several HIP previews of sections of text, so that students know what is expected.

Choose another chapter or section of text for students to preview on their own and talk to a partner about. Finally, give them an opportunity to individually preview and talk to their brains (see page 53) before reading.

Must-Do

Provide a piece of nonfiction text at students' independent reading level, and have students conduct their own HIP preview. If you want students to record their thinking, provide them with a copy of the Get HIP to Reading organizer on page 146.

Alpha-Boxes

Learning Goal: Students will be able to activate and organize prior knowledge before reading using an alphabet chart.

Alpha-box is the term coined by Linda Hoyt (1999) to describe an alphabetical chart that can be used both before and after reading to organize facts and details—and even during reading to collect notes. Reproduce the Alpha-Boxes Template on page 147 or create your own table with an alphabet letter in each box.

Introduce the text. You can have students do a HIP preview (see page 134), if you wish. Invite students to brainstorm words and ideas they already know about the topic. Record these words and phrases in the appropriate boxes on the chart, according to their initial letters. Be liberal about placing words and phrases on the chart—remember that the focus here is activating prior knowledge about the topic, not about filling every box.

Some teachers encourage students to make this routine a game by trying to generate at least one word for each box, but sometimes this leads to the inclusion of words that aren't particularly relevant to the topic and to ignoring important words for letters that are already represented. I simply encourage the students to see how many *key words* they can include in their organizer. It's sometimes necessary to talk about what constitutes a *key word*, although it's possible to build phrases using other starting letters.

After reading, revisit the chart and, with the students, highlight any words, phrases, and ideas encountered in the reading. There is likely to be more than one key word in many of the boxes and some boxes might not have any words. The important thing is generating words and phrases that are meaningful to the topic.

Alpha-Boxes - Snails

A antennas (see shell)	B breathe through hole under shell	C coiled shell	D deaf (no ears)	E eyes on top of feelers	F foot (long muscle) feelers
G gastropods	H herbivore	I	J	K	L land snails live long
M mucus muscle mollusk	N nocturnal	O	P people eat them	Q	R radula – ribbon-like tongue
S slimy shell slide slow	T tiny teeth (thousands) trail tentacles	U	V	W water	X, Y, Z (yucky)

After completing one or more alpha-boxes as a group, students can be given their own alpha-box to complete. For fluent readers, an alpha-box can be a convenient organizer for note-taking during reading as well as after reading.

Must-Do

- Provide each student with a copy of the partially completed alpha-box from the group. After reading the text, each student (or pair of students) must add a specified number of additional words and phrases to the chart.

- Have each student create a summary of what was read, using at least ten of the words/phrases on the completed chart. Encourage them to highlight the alpha-box words.
- Prepare a Jeopardy-style quiz game with the words in the boxes. Each student is assigned to write clues for three or four words on the game board.

During-Reading Routines

Most guided reading instruction with nonfiction text will focus on three main areas: comprehension, vocabulary, and text structure or features. Using sticky notes for instruction helps students track their thinking and become more meta-cognitive about their reading strategies.

Coding for Comprehension

This effective routine is adapted from the INSERT strategy developed by Vaughn and Estes (1986). It not only helps students comprehend nonfiction text, it also helps them *know* that they are comprehending. Coding simply involves using sticky notes to tab specific information in the text and using a coding system to identify those tabs.

Start with a simple coding system: *I knew this* and *I learned this*. Students tab facts that they already knew with a sticky note labeled with a check mark (✔) and facts that they learned with a sticky note labeled with a plus sign (✚).

Often I will have early readers read through the text once before coding it, then go back into the text with their sticky notes. Developing and fluent readers might be asked to code their comprehension on the first read.

As students become familiar with this process, we can add other codes. I like to add the "Wow!" code—a star (★)—for really interesting facts. For more sophisticated readers, I add a question mark (?) for "Can this be true?" If my students are going to become critical readers, they must learn to question what they read. (This is particularly important for the Internet generation, who are exposed to a glut of misleading information online.) I will often ask students to tab one fact that they might be sceptical of; then, after reading, they do research to verify or refute it.

Here is one routine for using the coding system:

1. Have students label four sticky notes with the four codes (see margin).
2. Designate a section of text to read. During the reading, students must use each of the codes once, and only once.
3. After reading, students share with a partner their tabbed facts. To develop oral reading fluency, have students read each of their tabbed facts aloud to their partner. Invite students to talk about which ideas they had the same experience with.
4. Have students remove their stickies and work with their partners to tab one fact *both* of them already knew, learned, questioned, and thought was fascinating.

When working with students at higher levels, you might have them place a long narrow sticky note down the right-hand margin of the page. As they read, they make one or more notations for every paragraph.

Must-Do

Provide students with another short section of text to read independently and have them individually use the four sticky tabs. If you would like to have a product for assessment, have them fold a paper in four and write and/or illustrate each of their facts in a section of the page.

Very Important Points

Learning Goal: Students will be able to distinguish key ideas from supporting details.

Distinguishing what's important from what's merely interesting is an important reading strategy, especially with nonfiction text. This routine, developed by Linda Hoyt (1999), guides students in thinking about distinguishing what's important from what's merely interesting in their reading.

We start by reviewing the difference between key ideas (what's important) and supporting details (what's interesting). Each student is asked to take four VIP sticky notes from his/her Reading Toolkit (see page 28). Students read the designated section of text and tab the four most-important ideas in the reading. Generally, I encourage students to do a cold read first, then go back into the text to identify the four key ideas. After reading, students share their VIPs and are expected to justify their choices. On a subsequent round of reading, I might give each *pair of students* six VIP tabs and ask them to collaborate on finding the six most important ideas. Limiting the number of VIPs helps students read the text more critically. Ultimately I want students to be able to identify the most important points in the reading, and to know why they are important.

Must-Do

- Students can be given another passage to read and tab with a required number of VIPs.
- Give students a T-chart labeled *Important* and *Interesting*. Have them reread the guided-reading passage or a new passage and record three or four points for each side of the chart.
- Have students use their VIPs to create a summary that includes each key idea. (See chapter 6 for a lesson on creating summaries.)

Gear Up for Reading

Learning Goal: Students will be able to adjust their reading speed according to the nature of the text and the purpose for reading.

We read at different rates and in different ways for different purposes. In fact, sometimes we even give ourselves permission to skip some text entirely if it doesn't meet our purpose for reading.

In some ways, reading is a bit like changing gears in a car (Carver, 1990). First gear is the slowest, most-powerful gear; we use it to read very difficult material or to memorize information. Second gear is the learning gear; we use it to read nonfiction. Third gear is the gear we use when reading narrative text, for pleasure or recreation. And fourth gear is the skimming and scanning gear we use to run our eyes over a piece of text to get a general sense of it or to locate a specific piece of information.

Set Your Reading Speed
First gear: for hard reading
Second gear: reading for learning
Third gear: reading for pleasure
Fourth gear: skimming or scanning

Review with students the different "gears" for reading, depending on the purpose. Practice using different reading rates and styles with sections of the guided reading text. (Chapter 6 contains a lesson on teaching students to skim, scan, or skip when reading.)

Must-Do

During independent reading, have students keep track of the gears they use when they read. Have them share their experiences at the next guided reading lesson.

Vocabulary Signals

Learning Goal: Students will be able to identify and use words that signal vocabulary support in the text.

Nonfiction text often contains supports for difficult vocabulary, such as definitions, restatements, or examples. In this lesson, students learn to look for *signal words* that indicate a connection between a difficult word and other words in the text.

- Some signal words tell you that the word will be defined or restated in another way:

  means, is defined as, may be described as, are known as
  that is, in other words, or

- Other words signal that examples of the unknown word are provided:

  such as, for example, like, for instance

- A last set of signal words provide comparisons and contrasts:

  just as, in the same way, similarly, like
  unlike, despite, however, on the other hand, in spite of, as opposed to, whereas, although,

With anchor charts, such as the signal word chart, it's more effective if students generate the word lists than if you provide the words for them. These charts can grow all year, as students discover more examples of the words.

Create a classroom anchor chart of signal words students encounter in their reading (see examples below). Continue to add to this chart as students discover more signal words. Use small-group guided reading to have students practice looking for signal words and using them to define or explain vocabulary and concepts in the text.

Signal Words Anchor Chart

Pay Attention! Words that signal that something is important:

Most of all…	*Remember that…*
The main thing….	*Especially important…*
Particularly valuable…	*It should be noted….*
Above all…	*In conclusion…*

Here's Why! Words that can signal cause and effect:

Because	*so*
Due to	*therefore*
In order that	*so that*
Consequently	*as a result*

It's a little fuzzy! Words that signal uncertainty:

Nearly	*appears to be*
Looked like	*reputed*
Alleged	*probably*
Sort of	*possible*
Might	*could*

We're changing Direction! Words that can signal a different position:

However	*Nevertheless*	*On the other hand*
Even though	*Otherwise*	*However,*
Conversely	*still*	*In contrast*
On the contrary	*rather than*	*whereas*

Choose a text that contains a few examples of words that signal clarification of unique or technical vocabulary. Give students one of the challenge words and ask them to find it in the text. They should read around the word (see page 81) to find other words that help indicate its meaning. Have students identify words that signal support for the challenge word. As students encounter new signal words, add them to the anchor chart.

Must-Do

Have students read another section of the guided-reading text or use a nonfiction text of their choice. Ask them to highlight three or four challenging words and look for supporting text to help define them. The chart on page 148 (or a paper folded into four columns) may be used to record the information.

Nonword Signals

Learning Goal: Students will be able to identify and use indicators, such as punctuation and text features, to aid comprehension of nonfiction text.

Not all signals in text are words. Punctuation also sends messages in print. Bold print, italics, and color can indicate particularly important information.

Nonverbal Signals include

- **bold** or colored print
- *italics*
- indentation
- exclamation point (!)
- underline or ~~strikethrough~~
- bullets
- numbers
- quotation marks (" ")
- arrows
- parentheses ( )
- dashes (–, —)
- icons

Have students go on a hunt in their guided-reading texts for text features and punctuation that send readers a particular message. They can use highlighting tape to draw attention to these features in the text. Talk about the messages each nonword signal conveys and how they help a reader.

Must-Do

Have students create a glossary of text features. Use a Poof Book (see page 160 in Appendix) or a three-column graphic organizer to record the signal, an example from the text, and what message it conveys in the text.

Fact or Opinion?

Learning Goal: Students will be able to distinguish between a factual statement and the author's opinion.

Many young readers—and a few older ones as well—have trouble distinguishing between a statement of fact and the writer's opinion. Find a statement in the guided-reading text that reflects an author's opinion and talk with students about the difference between a fact and an opinion.

Clues that Signal Opinions

- Opinions often use comparison words, such as *the most, the best, the least*, etc.
- Opinions are sometimes introduced with phrases of uncertainty, such as *it seems, I believe, it is probably*.

More sophisticated readers should be aware that an expert's opinion on a topic is more likely to have credibility than a novice's opinion. Also, whenever they identify an opinion, students should know that good writers support their opinions with strong evidence.

Have students identify an opinion in the text. Discuss how they know it is an opinion. Have students find support for the opinion. Is it credible? Is it reasonable? Encourage the students to be critical readers by attending to authors' opinions and the support they provide.

Must-Do

Provide students with copies of opinion or editorial text at their independent-reading level. Have them highlight *facts* with one color and *opinions* with another. At the next guided-reading session, revisit the text and have students explain why they identified the statements as they did.

Topic-Sentence Predictions

Learning Goal: Students will be able to identify topic sentences and use them to predict the information in the remainder of the text.

Remind the students that paragraphs in nonfiction text often (but not always) begin with a topic sentence that provides an overview of the information in that paragraph. (Topic sentences can appear at the end of the sentence or buried in the middle, rather than at the beginning. And many paragraphs have no topic sentence at all.)

Select a guided-reading text that contains paragraphs with clear topic sentences. After students have previewed the text, have them use a large sticky note to "underline" the topic sentence in the first paragraph and cover the rest of the paragraph. Read the sentence together and invite students' predictions about what information might be contained in the rest of the paragraph. Then have students read the rest of the paragraph to see if their predictions are confirmed. Be sure to model the kind of language that is expected: for example, *I think it's going to be about snails* is a superficial response; *I think it's going to explain what snails eat and how they chew* would be a more complete response.

Continue by having students use sticky notes to underline the topic sentence in the next paragraph with their sticky notes and talk to a partner (TTYN; see page 23) about what information might be in that paragraph. They read the paragraph to confirm or adjust the prediction, and continue with subsequent paragraphs.

Must-Do

Provide students with an independent-level text to work with or have them continue reading the guided-reading text. Have them use large sticky notes to cover each paragraph and predict the information based on the topic sentence. They can jot their predictions right on the sticky note or complete a graphic organizer, like the one on page 148. Be sure to model how to use the graphic organizer before expecting students to complete it on their own.

After-Reading Routines

There are many ways for students to respond to reading nonfiction text. Revisit the alpha-boxes (see page 135) or What We Think We Know charts (see page 133) to add more information or to confirm or reject anticipations. The Very Important Points routine (see page 137) can be used as a guide for summarizing the text.

Nonfiction reading can also lead to other research, as readers look for answers to their wonderings or simply seek to learn more about a topic. Often, we have students *synthesize* what they've learned by combining what was read with their own background knowledge and personal interpretations to create a new piece of visual or written text. Studies have shown that readers understand better and remember what they read longer when they write about their reading (Tierney & Shanahan, 1997).

Text Innovation: Pyramid Poems

A text innovation involves creating something new, an *innovation*, from an existing text. We might, for example, ask students to reframe a story as a newspaper article or to turn a piece of informational text into an acrostic poem. A popular framework based on Margaret Wise Brown's *The Important Book,* is often used with younger students (see sample below); see page 64 for the Important Thing Framework.

see page 64 for the Important Thing Framework.

> Snails   by Lisa
> The important thing about snails is that they carry ther shell on ther back.
> They have eyes on the end of ther feelers.
> They breath through a hole in ther shell.
> But the important thing about snails is that they carry ther house on ther back.

In this lesson, students use the language of the guided-reading text to construct a poem that starts with one word, the topic. Each subsequent line is one word longer than the previous line and is centred on the page to create a pyramid shape. The lines can include phrases or individual words; often unnecessary words (such as *the)* are omitted. Here is a student sample of a pyramid poem:

SNAILS
Silver trail
Live in shells
No eyes or nose
Body muscle called a foot
Thousands of tiny teeth grind food

Must-Do

This structure can be taught in the group and assigned as a must-do, or reinforced as a shared or interactive writing lesson. Invite students to choose a topic based on their guided-reading text and create their own pyramid poems.

Mind Maps

The mind map is a visual response to reading, as the students recount information learned about a topic through pictures, icons, and labels. This task can be introduced as an interactive experience, with students taking turns doing the sketching and labeling.

To create a mind map, start by drawing a picture or symbol of the topic or main idea in the centre of the page. Around the page, create pictures to repre-

---

Learning Goal: Students will be able to synthesize the information that was read by completing a written framework.

In an acrostic poem, the topic is written vertically, and each line of the poem starts with a letter from the topic word or words.

Learning Goal: Students will be able to present information learned from reading in a visual form.

sent the information learned about the topic. Students might be asked to provide written labels for their pictures.

Must-Do

Provide students with an informational text to read, and have them create individual mind maps (see sample below). Remember that the purpose of this exercise is to communicate information visually, not to draw the prettiest pictures! At the next guided reading session, students should be given an opportunity to share and explain their mind maps.

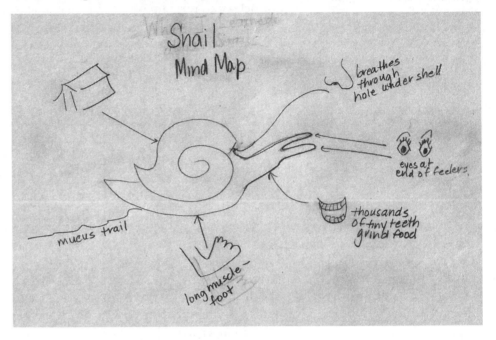

Five False Facts

Learning Goal: Students will be able to gather facts on a topic and distinguish accurate from inaccurate facts.

From the guided-reading text, generate a collection of facts about the topic. You might want to use facts from the What We Think We Know chart (see page 133) or the alpha-boxes (see page 135). Talk with students about how you can turn around a true fact to make it into a false fact. For example, you might take a true fact like *The snail's body consists of a muscle called a foot* and flip it to *Snails have two feet at the end of their bodies.*

When students have generated some true and false facts, discuss how they might distinguish a fact that is true from one that is not when they are reading.

Must-Do

This after-reading response might require students to conduct research beyond the guided-reading text. Have students gather ten interesting facts about the topic, then flip five of the facts into "false facts." They can each fact on an index card and illustrate them, if desired. For example, you might take *Snails have thousands of tiny teeth to grind up their food* and turn it into *Snails do not have teeth and swallow their food whole.* On the back of the card, students explain whether the fact is true or false; if it is false, they add the true fact. Have students trade cards and try to identify their partner's false facts from looking at only the front of the cards.

Vocabulary Sorts

Learning Goal: Students will be able to identify relationships among new and known words.

The same word-solving strategies and activities used with narrative text can be used with informational text. Word hunts, word sorts, and word-building are every bit as useful in reading nonfiction as in fiction reading. Alpha-boxes (see page 147 for template) and signal words (page 138) are also great vocabulary tools.

Vocabulary sorts can be conducted as a prereading exercise, with teacher-selected words, but I prefer to have students choose the words and work with them after reading. If you have completed alpha-boxes with your students, you will already have a collection of vocabulary words. With students, generate a list of 10 to 12 words from the guided-reading text. Start by talking about which words go together and why. Then discuss ways that groups of words can be sorted into categories. (Ultimately, I require students to sort the words by meaning rather than by letter or syllable features.)

Here is a word-sorting routine that works for a variety of reading experiences:

1. Gather a collection of at least eight to ten words related to the topic from the guided-reading text.
2. Have students work in pairs or small groups to sort the words into at least two categories. There might be several categories but there must be at least two words in each. Some words might fit into more than one group.
3. Students give a name to each group to explain how the words are related.
4. Extend the experience by inviting students to generate at least one word, not from the text, that could be added to each group.

There are no right or wrong answers for this activity, as long as students can reasonably justify their groupings.

Must-Do

Have students do another word hunt from the guided-reading text or provide each pair of students with another set of vocabulary cards to sort and label, following the same process. You might have them choose two or three words to create Vocabulary Squares (see page 83.)

Key Word Summaries

Learning Goal: Students will be able to identify key words from a passage.

When we retell what we've read, we try to recall every single detail. When we summarize, we record only key ideas. One way to help students make the transition from retelling to summarizing is to limit the number of key words from the text. Here are two routines for locating key words in the text.

1. Key Word Highlights

Provide students with short pieces of highlighting tape in their Reading Toolkits. After they have read a short designated section of text, they should highlight three to five important words in the text. Then they turn to a partner and summarize what they have read, using the highlighted words in their summaries.

2. Two-Word Summaries

In this routine, developed by Linda Hoyt (2009), readers select two key words from each paragraph to use in constructing a summary of the text. Together, read a sentence or paragraph from the guided-reading text. Instruct students to choose two words to help them remember that detail. Continue with the next sentence. After reading a paragraph (or a page, depending on the readers and the text), have students cover the text and use only their two-word summaries to retell what was read.

Must-Do

Have students continue this routine in partners, reading on the same guided-reading text or using a different text that is at their independent-reading level. Partners read a page independently, highlighting three to five words, then stop and share their highlighted words with each other, summarizing the text orally or in writing, using those vocabulary words.

Oral Reading Fluency

The same techniques and activities used to support oral reading fluency in narrative text can also be used for informational text. Provide practice in automatic word recognition, phrasing, punctuation, pacing, and expression. Remember that fluency should be a habit, not an event. Build oral reading experiences into the lesson routine by having students read aloud sections of text after reading them silently.

Must-Do

Why not a performance reading of nonfiction? Divide students into pairs to practice dramatically reading an assigned piece of short text (between a paragraph and a page in length). Encourage them to overdramatize! They need to convey to other students that this is absolutely the most fascinating piece of information they will ever encounter. Performances are done at the next guided reading session.

Learning Goal: Students will be able to read informational material with phrasing and expression.

Sample Guided Reading Lesson Plan with Nonfiction Text

Group: Early Developing Level

Title	Learning Goals
Snails	Comprehension: getting information from texts; self-monitoring comprehension Word Study: Context clues

Text/Book Introduction

Preview:

This is an information book about snails. What do we know about information books? How are they different from story books?

Prior Knowledge:

Let's think about what we already know – or what we think we know about snails. Complete a What We Think We Know chart together.

Purpose:

Today, as you read, you need to think about all the facts about snails. Use the sticky strips in your Reading Toolkit. When you read a fact that you already knew, tab it with a green sticky strip. When you read a fact that you didn't know but you learned, tab it with a yellow sticky strip.

Day 1	Must-Do
• Book introduction: What We Think We Know chart • First reading: tab "knew" with green stickies and "new" with yellow stickies • If time, partner share	4-square foldable: 2 things I already knew, 2 things I learned
Day 2	**Must-Do**
• Second reading: read in partners • Partner share must-do squares • Revisit WWTWK charts to add what we learned and what we wonder	Computer reading in pairs – website on snails: www.kiddyhouse.com/snails.
Day 3	**Must-Do**
• *Take turns reading your most interesting page aloud* • Focus on context clues: *Read around the word "mucus" and highlight any words that help you guess what mucus means.* • Model the mind map	Create a mind map about snails using pictures and labels

Get HIP to Reading

Headings: What are two things you know from the headings?

1. _____

    _____

2. _____

    _____

Introduction:

This reading is going to be about _____

_____

_____ .

I predict that it will tell _____

_____

_____ .

I'm wondering _____

_____

_____ .

Pictures: What are two things you've learned from the pictures?

1. _____

    _____

2. _____

    _____

Alpha-Box Template

A	**B**	**C**	**D**
E	**F**	**G**	**H**
I	**J**	**K**	**L**
M	**N**	**O**	**P**
Q	**R**	**S**	**T**
U	**V**	**W**	**XYZ**

Pembroke Publishers ©2012 *Guiding Readers* by Lori Jamison Rog ISBN 978-1-55138-273-9

Meaning of the Word

Look for examples of signal words in your reading and record them in the chart.

Vocabulary Word	Signal Word	Signal Word or Phrase	How the Signal Word Helped

Topic-Sentence Predictions

Topic Sentence	I think this paragraph will include the following information	This paragraph actually included the following information

Pembroke Publishers ©2012 *Guiding Readers* by Lori Jamison Rog ISBN 978-1-55138-273-9

9

Functional Reading

Think about the reading you've done over the past day or two. Chances are it involved reading directions or a recipe, a map or a menu, the ingredients on a package, a TV schedule or a flyer from your local grocery store. You've likely done some of this reading on a computer or other electronic device, if your household is among the 80% of the population of North America with Internet access, and that spends an average of 18 hours a week online (Internet World Stats, 2011). This type of reading is referred to as *functional reading*, the kind of reading we do essentially to function in the world, day to day.

Even as we've strived to increase our students' exposure to informational texts in the guided-reading program, we know there are many more forms of nonfiction in our world. In fact, the kind of reading we do most in life is actually the kind least taught in schools! Why is it that so many adults have to rely on their children to help them program the PVR or burn a CD? Knowing how to do these things involves being able to understand and follow written directions. And then there are all the other forms of print and nonprint media, from brochures to street signs to maps to websites, that are designed to help us function in life. The guided reading lesson is an ideal time to reinforce the strategies needed to access those very important reading forms, with accessible text and teacher support in small groups.

Guided reading with real-world texts is likely to look a little different from instruction with more conventional educational texts. For one thing, it is more difficult to find accessible texts at our students' instructional-reading levels. That means we might have to compromise on the level of difficulty by offering more scaffolding in the text introduction or by expecting students to read only portions of the text independently. For example, when reading a TV schedule, we might help with the names of shows, but expect students to navigate the table of times and channels. We are likely to be doing more teaching and scaffolding during the reading than we would in a traditional guided reading lesson, but small-group time is the ideal opportunity to provide the support that enables students to read the world around them.

Selecting Texts for Guided Reading

Texts for functional reading can be found all around us! Copy some recipes for familiar foods. Download a bus schedule or order form from the Internet. The next time you're on vacation, grab some travel brochures from a hotel lobby. Get students to help by looking for examples of how-to reading in their own homes: rules for games, manuals for appliances, instructions for making something. Food packaging is also an important source of environmental print for guided reading—from ingredients to cooking instructions.

Reference materials, such as dictionaries, glossaries, tables of contents, and even the almost-obsolete telephone book, are forms of functional text, as are forms, such as applications, contest entries, or banking information. We often teach students how to use the index in an informational book, but how often do we teach them to use the newspaper's index? How often do we look for authentic functional writing tasks, such as filling out an application for a library card? Small-group reading is an excellent structure for helping young readers practice the kinds of reading they need to do in order to operate in a literate world.

Making the reader–text match will be a little trickier with real-world writing than with the usual leveled books. After all, these are authentic texts, not stories created to support developing readers. Most functional text will not stand up to the usual leveling and readability criteria. That means we have to use our professional judgment about how much we want students to be able to read on their own and how much support we will provide. Published materials that introduce functional text forms for beginning readers are hard to find. In many cases, it will be easier and more efficient to simply create your own text than to search for an appropriate text for young readers. For example, you can easily create a book of traffic signs from clipart or by walking around your neighborhood with a camera. The level of the text will be based on the amount and type of print you choose to put on the page. (See the examples on page 151.)

Environmental Print for Beginning Readers

Most functional print was not intended to be read by emergent and early readers. However, we know that even preschoolers can identify familiar brand names from everyday labels, such as those on toothpaste, snacks, and fast food. They know traffic signs around them. They even recognize TV schedules, recipes, and menus (see student sample in margin). We can take advantage of that knowledge about and interest in the print around them to teach many lessons on letters, sounds, and print features.

There are a variety of ways we can support the development of letter, word, and print-feature understandings through environmental print. For example, children who recognize the word "Crest" on the toothpaste tube will not necessarily recognize it in plastic letters or standard print. Matching, sorting, and manipulating print can all be practiced and reinforced in small-group settings. Invite families to help you gather a collection of labels, signs, and packaging, or print copies from Internet images or other sources. Guided reading routines with environmental print might include the following:

- Matching words and letters in different fonts, sizes, and colors
- Matching pictures and words
- Comparing letters on different labels: Which are the same? Which are different?
- Sorting by initial consonants, syllables, final consonants, etc.
- Hunting for specific letters and letter patterns

Reading for Information
- TV listings
- advertisements
- bus schedules
- weather charts
- menus
- websites
- travel brochures

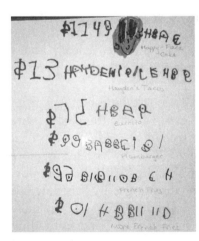

For downloadable images of environmental print items, see www.hubbardscupboard.org/i_can_read_.html

- Reinforcing letter patterns, such as blends, double letters, vowel combinations, and rimes
- Sorting by plurals and singular words
- Looking for inflectional endings: *-ed*, *-ing*, *-s*
- Sorting by context (e.g., things you eat, things you do, places you go)
- Creating riddles to be answered by different environmental print items

Samples of Emergent-Level Text

Samples of Early-Level Text

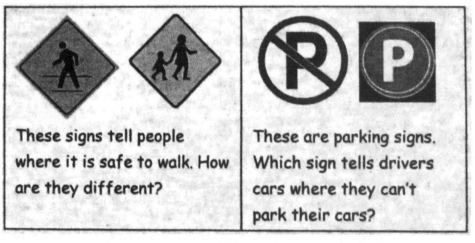

Samples of Developing-Level Text

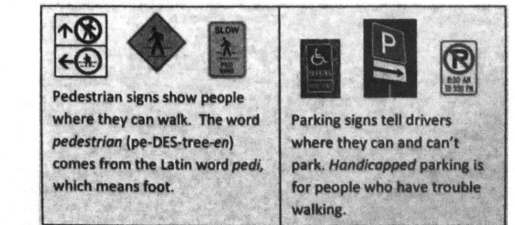

Lesson Routines

Many of the routines in this chapter are more teacher-directed than others in the book. You might introduce them as shared reading before practicing during small-group instruction. However, the small-group setting is ideal for having students work with unique forms as we scaffold and reinforce their learning.

Reading to Follow Directions

Learning Goal: Students will be able to read a map to follow directions.

From a mapping website, print a map of a familiar area, such as a route from your school to a nearby park or shopping centre. (Use the "walking" feature on the site.) Provide each student with a copy of the map. In small groups, students can view the map online as well, but hard copies enable students to highlight and mark the page. Before reading, discuss with the students the various symbols on the map; for example:

- Direction arrows
- Starting and ending symbols
- Symbols for attractions, such as restaurants or shopping
- Symbols for driving, walking, or public transportation

Texts for Reading to Follow Directions
- recipes and cooking instructions
- craft and hobby instructions
- directions on a map
- instructions for playing a game
- appliance manuals
- any how-to reading

Talk about why the maps contain symbols rather than, or in addition to, words. Look at verbal directions in the form of imperative sentences, or commands. Discuss the words that appear over and over again. Preteach any unfamiliar words.

Invite students to take a few minutes to look at the map and talk about what they see. They might point out street names they recognize or familiar features, such as schools, churches, or parks. Point out street names the students don't recognize, or give clues for the students to figure them out. If there are other identifiable features on the map, point them out.

Have students put their finger on the starting point (often a green dot). Together, read each step and track the route on the map with fingers.

Must-Do

1. Provide directions from the school to another site that is not marked on the map. Have students mark the map with the route described. Where do they end up?
2. Provide students with a route marked on a map, but without written directions. Have them write out the directions.
3. Provide students with a map so they can mark the directions *and* the route on the map independently.

Complete a Craft

Learning Goal: Students will be able to follow written directions to complete a craft.

The best way to assess students' comprehension of procedural text is to see how well they can perform the procedure.

Look at the directions and talk about the features of the text form: description of the finished product, materials required, steps in making the craft. Some instructions include the time required to complete the task.

You might spend some time on the unique structure of the imperative sentence; i.e., the command. Students have learned by now that a sentence needs a *who or what* and an *is or does*. In these sentences, there is a doing part—e.g., "cut the paper", "fold in half"—but there is no name part. The subject of the sentence is "you," the reader, the person who is using the directions. It doesn't have to be stated in the sentence; it is understood. Also note that each sentence starts with a verb.

Another notable feature of this text form is the spareness of language. Note that there are no "Wow!" words here, no figurative or fancy language. It's important that the directions be clear and specific.

As they read, have students highlight words they aren't sure of, using highlighting pens or tape. You might have them code their highlights: yellow for "I don't know what this word means" and green for "I'm not sure what this word means, but I think I can figure it out from the passage." Together, review these words before having students complete the craft. Make sure the students understand all the text before completing the task independently.

Must-Do

After analyzing the directions in guided reading, have students work individually or in pairs to follow the directions to complete the craft. In the next guided-reading session, talk about which directions were easy and which were harder to follow, and how the directions might have explained the step more clearly.

Signs of the Times

Learning Goal: Students will be able to interpret signs in public areas.

Public information signs in the community are essential functional reading tasks. The photo here shows a sign from a dog-walking park that could be an entire guided reading lesson by the time you examine the text, the vocabulary, and the map.

Invite students to read as much as they can of the sign. Help them with unfamiliar words.

Areas for guided reading discussion might include these prompts:

- What is the purpose of signs like this? What other signs do you know that help public safety?
- Why is one section of the map red and the rest yellow? What do those colors represent?
- What do you think a "code of conduct" is and why should we refer to it?
- Why do you think people are told they should "avoid active playing areas"?
- Do you think an off-leash area for dogs is a good idea?
- What does "under control" mean?

Must-Do

Make the reading–writing connection. Have students create a sign that gives rules for dogs in the school playground. They should include color-coding, a map, and directions.

Read a Website

Learning Goal: Students will be able to navigate the main features of an Internet website.

Internet sites are the quintessential example of nonlinear reading. Most sites have information in different places on the page. We click on links to move to other pages, and then can go back to the original page or move on to other pages. This lesson sequence enables us to work interactively with small groups of students to study a unique text form that is often read but rarely taught.

There are many lessons that should be explicitly taught in terms of Internet use, including searching online, using a browser, and Internet safety. In this sample lesson sequence, we will focus on

This lesson sequence has not been broken into individual sessions, but the entire numbered set of lessons will take place over several 18-minute sessions.

- features of a website
- reading around the page
- bouncing around the Net

Choose an age- and reading-level-appropriate website. It might be difficult to find web pages at an appropriate reading level for early readers, so you will have to decide how much scaffolding you are prepared to do and how much you want students to be able to read on their own. There are many good websites for kids, such as children's magazine or public TV websites. Unfortunately—or not—most of them have advertising, but even advertising can offer an opportunity to teach young students to be critical readers and distinguish promotional material from facts.

An excellent interactive website that takes students through an introduction to Internet use is www.teachingideas.co.uk/welcome/start.htm

1. Ironic (and perhaps archaic) as it may seem, I like to start by printing a webshot of the page. (Your favorite search engine will help you find *functional text* to help you create a webshot, if you don't know how.) In this way, students will be able to use markers to mark up the page, circle important text features, and highlight key information.
2. Start by asking students to preview the page and to circle the first feature they notice. Talk about what that feature is called (title, logo, graphics, information, etc.) and why it stood out. (It may very well be different features for different students.) Have them write number *1* in the circle, then go on to identify the second feature that they notice. Go through the same process with about five text features, then tell students to connect the circles in order. This provides a very vivid representation of nonlinear reading. When we read fiction books, we generally read top to bottom and left to right. When we read a web page, our eyes often bounce around to different parts of the page. Take time to talk about the parts that they *didn't* notice—and why not.

   Make sure that students have identified and named key features of the website. Some of the features that a website might contain include

   - navigation bar(s)
   - web address (URL)
   - blog
   - contact form
   - title and/or logo
   - graphics
   - fonts in different styles, colors, sizes

- things to buy
- interactive surveys
- advertising

Must-Do

Provide students with a website you have already screened. Have them use a graphic organizer like the one below to identify each of the features on the chart and explain what information is provided on the website. For example, beside *URL*, they would write the actual address of the site; beside *Picture*, they would describe a picture on the site.

Text Feature	*What it says*
URL	
Logo and/or Title	
Text that looks interesting or unusual	
Interactive Survey	
Picture	
Symbol or Icon	
Advertisement	

3. Now it's time to guide students through the actual website. Ideally, you will have enough computers for each student to have his/her own monitor and keyboard. Otherwise, it will be necessary for students to work in pairs. Start by identifying the text features that were noted on the webshots. Ask questions about the content on the page for students to answer. Encourage them to generate questions as well.

4. When students are looking for specific information or text features, point out that they have to bounce their eyes all over the page. The way we read a webpage is affected by our purpose for reading. When we're looking for specific information, we *scan* by running our eyes quickly over the page to focus on a keyword. When we want a general sense of what the website is about, we *skim* by running our eyes quickly over the text to get the gist, almost like previewing the page. (If this were a webpage, I could create a hyperlink to Get HIP to Reading. Because it's a book, I just have to tell you to go back to page 134.) Sometimes we even *skip* certain information that we know doesn't fit our purpose. It's important that students be conscious of this reading action. (See Gear Up for Reading on page 137.)

Hyperlinks, or simply *links*, are the bridges between one webpage and another. *Hypertext* is the text (or image or icon) on the page that contains the link; when you click on it, it takes you to another page or document. Sometimes just using the mouse to hover over hypertext will pop up a definition or additional information.

- Hyperlinks within text are often (but not always) underlined.
- Hyperlinks can be words or pictures. Sometimes different parts of the same picture can have different hyperlinks.
- If you move your cursor over a hyperlink, it will change to the shape of a hand.
- If you click on a hyperlink, it will take you to a different page.

5. Tell students that the Internet is a huge collection of computers around the world that share information. From one page on the worldwide web (www), it's possible to link to millions of other pages of information, pictures, movies, and the like. That's why readers need to know more than how to read a single webpage; they need to know how to "bounce around" on the worldwide web to many different websites.

For this lesson, students will need computer access to a pre-selected website. Start by visiting the navigation bar, which usually links to other parts of the same website. Explain to the students what a *hyperlink* (or simply *link*) is. Point out some of the links and invite students to click on them. Draw their attention to the Back button (a left facing arrow on the left-hand corner of the toolbar) that takes you back to the page you were on just previously. Prepare some questions ahead of time for students to research on the site. Talk about how to decide whether to click on a hyperlink or not.

Must-Do

Have students complete a Webquest: A webquest is a practical application of students' Internet reading skills. Students must answer a set of questions or complete a task using information from the Internet. Often there is a "hook," such as a game or treasure hunt. You can create your own webquests or use one of the many teacher-prepared webquests on the Internet.

Read a Brochure

Many of us pick up brochures for local attractions when we're traveling, but how often do we use these brochures to teach our students about functional reading? Brochures from exotic travels can be fun to study, but children are more engaged by attractions right in their neighborhood.

Brochures contain a variety of text features for students to study, such as

- different fonts, colors, size of print
- headings and subheadings
- "loaded" words (see page 157)
- time schedules
- fee schedules
- maps
- pictures and other visuals

Talk about what kinds of information a person might be seeking in a brochure; for example, what hours the attraction is open, how much it costs, where it is, and what you can see and do. Have students hunt in their brochures for this information and label each relevant section with a sticky note.

Webquest 101 (www2.teachersfirst.com/summer/webquest/quest-b.shtml) offers a tutorial for creating curriculum-based websites, but an Internet search will generate many prepared webquests for students of all ages and reading levels.

Learning Goal: Students will be able to locate relevant information from a travel brochure.

See page 158 for a lesson sequence for studying a brochure from the Houston Zoo.

Must-Do

Provide students with a different brochure and have them identify key information by moving the sticky notes from the brochure used in guided reading to the new brochure.

Loaded Words

Learning Goal: Students will be able to identify words that are intended to persuade or cause emotion in a reader.

Loaded words are words that are deliberately used to evoke emotion in a reader. They can be words that generate positive feelings, like *better* or *healthy,* or words that generate negative feelings, like *polluted* or *danger.* Writers of persuasive text often use loaded words to try to make their readers have strong feelings about the topic. Provide students with a list of words, such as *exciting, litter, safe, wild, nature.* Have them talk to a partner about whether these words evoke positive, negative, or neutral emotions.

When students understand the concept, have them go into a travel brochure and highlight words that they consider to be loaded. After reading, talk about how these words act on our emotions to persuade us to think a certain way.

Must-Do

Provide students with a short piece of persuasive text at their independent-reading levels. Have them make a list of loaded words and sort them according to whether they are positive or negative.

Sample Guided Reading Lesson Plan with Functional Text

Group: Fluent Level

Text	**Learning Goals**
Houston Zoo Brochure	Comprehension • understanding the text structure of a brochure • gathering information from a brochure • noting advertising techniques Word Study • loaded words

Book Introduction

Preview:

We've been talking about information we get from brochures. Often interesting places like museums and theme parks create brochures to make people want to visit them. Today we're going to look at a brochure for the Houston Zoo.

Prior Knowledge:

What kinds of information would you need or want to know if you were thinking about going to the Houston Zoo? Generate a list of questions with the group.

Purpose:

Let's read to see if this brochure will tell us what we want and need to know.

Day 1	**Must-Do**
• Text introduction: *Make a list of things you want/need to know if you are going to the zoo. Make a list of questions.* • Provide each student with a copy of the brochure. Talk about the different text features: bold print, photographs, map, etc. • Have students read for the required information to answer the questions	Have students choose 4–5 questions from the list and write them on sticky notes. They place the sticky notes on their brochures in the places where the answers are found.
Day 2	**Must-Do**
• Revisit must-do. *Is any information missing? How might you find that information? What additional information does the brochure provide that you find interesting? What information do you think is unnecessary?* • Explain about loaded words that generate emotion. Word Hunt: Have students highlight five loaded words that make them want to visit the zoo.	Provide students with a different brochure. Have them write four key questions from the group list on sticky notes and place them on the answers to the questions. Have them highlight three loaded words.

Appendix: Reproducibles and Tools

The following tips, tools, and folded graphic organizers are referred to in the guided-reading routines in the text, but can be used for a variety of purposes.

Milk-Carton Dice

1. To make safe, inexpensive easy-to-use dice, use two clean milk cartons. Cut each one down so the height is equal to the length and width (i.e., cube- sized).

2. Tuck one carton inside the other (it might help to slice along the folds of the inside carton) with open sides together to form a cube.

3. Cover the cube with paper and add any labels you choose.

Four-Square Organizer

This is one of the simplest folded organizers.

1. Fold a square or rectangular piece of paper in four.
2. Lay the paper on the table so the folded point (no raw edges) is in the bottom right corner.
3. Fold that corner up to make a triangle.

4. When the paper is unfolded, you have four squares with a diamond in the centre.
5. You can make an additional folded organizer by folding the bottom right-hand corner twice. This gives a four-square organizer with two diamonds in the middle or with an extra writing section in each of the four corners.

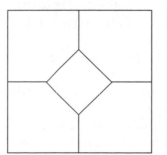
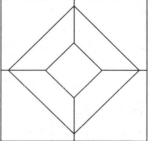

Poof Book

1. Use any size of paper. Fold it once in half lengthwise (hotdog fold) and once in half width-wise (hamburger fold). When you unfold the paper, it will be divided into four sections.
2. Make a shutter fold by folding both edges toward the middle, just like a shutter on a window. When you put the paper on the table, it should look like a *W*.

3. Use scissors to cut (or carefully tear) a line through both sides of the centre (hotdog) fold to the bottom of the folds.

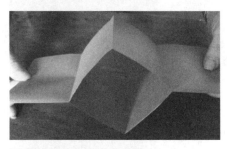

4. Refold the paper along the long (hotdog) fold. You'll see how the middle "poofs" out.

5. Grab both ends and push them toward the middle. The book will fold naturally.

Foldable Comparison Chart

Who ever said that Venn diagrams had to be round? Rectangular shapes offer much more space for writing.

1. Cut a sheet of 8" ×11" paper in half horizontally and cut strips that are 11 inches wide by 4 inches high.
2. Make a shutter fold by folding both edges in so that they meet in the middle (like shutters on a window). Do not make the centre fold.
3. When unfolded, the paper will have two smaller sections on either end, to itemize the features of the individuals, and a large section in the middle for the features they have in common.
4. When folded in, the outside of the two flaps can be used to identify the individual items, stories, or characters that are being compared.

Flap Book

Lift-the-flap books can have as many flaps as you choose. This sample uses four flaps, which are easy to fold, but you can have as few or as many flaps as you want.

1. Fold a piece of paper in half lengthwise (hotdog fold).
2. Then fold it in half crosswise (hamburger fold) twice, so that the paper is folded in eight.
3. Unfold the hamburger folds. Place the paper in front of you with the fold at the top and the opening at the bottom.

4. Cut on each top fold line to the centre fold, so that the bottom is one solid piece and the top consists of four flaps.

5. The flap book can be used horizontally or vertically.

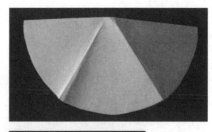

Circular Foldable

Create circular foldables using thin paper plates.

1. Fold paper plates in half, then in thirds, to create six sections. Here's a trick for folding the round shape in thirds: roll the half-round into a cone shape so the edges overlap completely, then crease it down to form thirds.
2. While the circle is folded, fold up the point. This will make a hexagonal shape in the middle when it's unfolded.

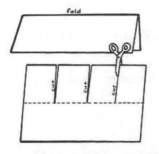

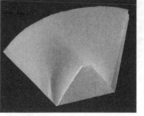

3. Unfold the circle and you have six equal parts with a hexagon in the middle.

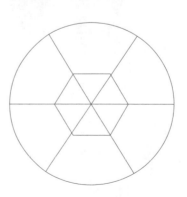

Tips for Reading Manipulatives

Many ordinary items from the dollar or discount store make useful reading manipulatives to encourage students to go back into the text to focus on words, letters, and patterns. Here are some of my favorites. I'm sure you can find more!

Pointers can be used for tracking words or pointing out individual letter features:

- fancy pencils, especially with fancy erasers, left unsharpened
- chopsticks
- cocktail swizzle sticks

Reading Fingers: Halloween is a good time to buy plastic "witch fingers" that the students can use for tracking print.

Word/Letter Framers: Anything with a hole in it can be used to frame letters and words:

- fly swatter with a hole cut in the centre
- magnifying glass
- bubble wand

Small Plastic Rulers can be used as sliders, for readers to slide under the line as they read.

"Reading" Glasses: funny plastic eyeglasses or regular glasses with the lenses removed

Plastic Plates can be used as individual whiteboards with dry-erase markers; little gloves can be used as erasers.

Metal Stove-burner Covers for holding magnetic (or non-magnetic) letters. The lip keeps the letters in place.

Alphabet Letters: magnetic, plastic, pasta, foam

Notebooks and Note Paper

Sticky Notes: Stock up on various shapes and sizes; look for unusual shapes, like arrows or stars. Translucent stickies can be used for highlighting words and ideas in texts.

Craft Sticks: Use as partner sticks by coloring one end of each stick with marker, so that there are two of each color. Each student draws a partner stick and is automatically paired with the student who draws the same color.

Timers: Try to find timers with a loud ring, to mark the end of the 18-minute lesson. Electronic or sand timers can also be used for partner work, such as buddy reading.

Hand Clappers: Take them apart and use each hand to "put your hand on a word."

Bingo Chips and Game Pieces can be used for word bingo games or finding words in a text. Translucent bingo chips can be used on overhead projectors for highlighting individual words and letters

Shower Curtain Liners can be sectioned and written on to make enlarged game boards. Bean bags can be tossed onto the game boards to identify high-frequency words, letter patterns, or word families.

Hats/Visors/Crowns/Tiaras: Headwear can serve a variety of purposes, such as identifying the leader of the day. If you don't want to use head-gear, colored scrunchies on the wrist can identify group members or special roles.

Storage Containers: Four or five stackable bins (one for each guided-reading group) can be used to store all the materials for that group.

Attention-getters:

- whistles (especially train whistles)
- wind chimes
- hand clappers

Dice in Plastic Pill Containers: Many games and activities involve the roll of the dice. Get clear plastic pill containers— large enough to shake the dice and see the number face through the clear part—from the local pharmacy. This prevents the dice from rolling away!

Game Board and Spinner Templates

Pembroke Publishers ©2012 *Guiding Readers* by Lori Jamison Rog ISBN 978-1-55138-273-9

Resources

Allington, R. (2006) *What Really Matters for Struggling Readers: Designing research-based programs,* 2nd ed. Boston, MA: Pearson

Allington, R. (2005) "Urgency and instructional time" *Reading Today,* August, 23(1), 17.

Baumann, J. F. & Ivey, G. (1997) "Delicate Balances: Striving for curricular and instructional equilibrium in a second-grade, literature/strategy-based classroom" *Reading Research Quarterly,* 32(3), 244–275.

Beers, K. (2003) *When Kids Can't Read.* Portsmouth, NH: Heinemann

Benson, V. & Cummins, C. (2004) *The Power of Retelling.* New York, NY: Wright Group-McGraw Hill.

Betts, E. (1946) *Foundations of Reading Instruction.* New York, NY: American Book Company.

Biancarosa, C. & Snow, C. E. (2006) *Reading Next—A vision for action and research in middle and high school literacy: A report to Carnegie Corporation of New York,* 2nd ed. Washington, DC: Alliance for Excellent Education.

Bouchey, G. & Moser, J. (2005) *The Daily Five.* Portland, ME: Stenhouse.

Burkins, J. & Croft, M. (2010) *Preventing Misguided Reading: New strategies for guided reading teachers.* Newark, DE: International Reading Association.

Carver, R. (1990) *Reading Rate: a review of research and theory.* Boston, MA: Academic Press.

Clay, M. (2002) *Running Records for Classroom Teachers.* Portsmouth, NH: Heinemann.

Cotton, K. (1988) *Classroom Questioning.* Education Northwest School Improvement Research Series at educationnorthwest.org/webfm_send/569

Cuban, L. (1993) *How Teachers Taught: Constancy and change in American classrooms: 1980–1990,* 2nd ed. New York, NY: Longman.

Cunningham, P. & Hall, D. (1998) *Month-by-Month Phonics for Upper Grades.* Greensboro, NC: Carson-Dellosa.

Cunningham, P. M. & Cunningham, J. W. (1992) "Making Words: Enhancing the invented spelling-decoding connection" *Reading Teacher,* 46, 106–115.

Diller, D. (2003) *Literacy Work Stations.* Portland, ME: Stenhouse.

Duke, N. K. (2000) "3.6 minutes per day: The scarcity of informational texts in first grade" *Reading Research Quarterly,* 35, 202–224.

Duke, N. K. & Pearson, D. (2002) "Effective Practices for Developing Reading Comprehension" in A. E. Farstrup & S. J. Samuels (eds.) *What Research Has To Say About Reading Instruction,* 3rd ed. (205–242). Newark, DE: International Reading Association.

Fawson, P. C. & Reutzel, R. (2000) "But I only have a basal: Implementing GR in early grades" *Reading Teacher,* 54, 84–98.

Fisher, P. & Blachowicz, C. (2005) "Vocabulary instruction in a remedial setting" *Reading and Writing Quarterly,* 21, 281–300.

Fountas, I. & Pinnell, G. (1996) *Guided Reading.* Portsmouth, NH: Heinemann.

Gambrell, L. B. & Koskinen, P. S. (2002) "Imagery: A strategy for enhancing comprehension" in C. C. Block & M. Pressley (eds.) *Comprehension instruction: Research-based practices* (305–318). New York, NY: Guilford.

Gear, A. (2006) *Reading Power.* Markham, ON: Pembroke

Goldsmith, A. (2007) "Why Kids Need Series Books" American Association of School Librarians Sept/October at /www.ala.org/ala/mgrps/divs/aasl/aasl-pubsandjournals/knowledgequest/kqwebarchives/v36/361/361goldsmith_.cfm

Honig, B. et al. (2000) *Teaching Reading Sourcebook: For kindergarten through eighth grade.* Novato, CA: Arena Press.

Hoyt, L. (2009) *Revisit, Reflect, Retell: Time-tested strategies for teaching reading comprehension*. Portsmouth, NH: Heinemann.

Iaquinta, A. (2006) "Guided Reading: A research-based response to the challenges of early reading instruction" *Early Childhood Education Journal*, 33:6, 413–418

Internet World Stats (2011) at http://www.internetworldstats.com/stats.htm

Jamison Rog, L. (2010) *Marvelous Minilessons for Teaching Intermediate Writing, Grades 4–6*. Newark, DE: International Reading Association.

Jamison Rog, L. & Burton, W. (2000/2001) "Matching Readers and Texts" *The Reading Teacher*, December 2000–January 2001.

Kelly, P. R. & Neal, J. C. (1998) "Keeping the Processing Easy at Higher Levels of Text Reading" *The Running Record*, 11(1), 1–10.

Klingner, J. & Vaughn, S. (1999) "Promoting Reading Comprehension: English acquisition and content learning through Collaborative Strategic Reading (CSR)" *The Reading Teacher*, 52 (7), 738–747.

Kosanovich, M., Ladinsky, K., Nelson, L. & Torgeson, J. (2006) "Differentiated reading instruction: small group alternative lesson structures for all students" Florida Center for Reading Research at www.fcrr.org

Langer, J. A. (1984) "Examining Background Knowledge and Text Comprehension" *Reading Research Quarterly*, 19(4), 468–481.

Lyman, F. (1987) "Think-Pair-Share: An expanding teaching technique" *MAA-CIE Cooperative News*, 1, 1–2.

McGee, L. & Richgels, D. (2011) *Literacy's Beginnings: Supporting young readers and writers*. Boston, MA: Allyn & Bacon.

McGregor, T. (2007) *Comprehension Connections: Bridges to strategic reading*. Portsmouth, NH: Heinemann.

McKenna, M. (2002) *Help for Struggling Readers: Strategies for grades 3–8*. New York, NY: Guilford.

Mooney, M. (1988) *Developing Life-long Readers*. Katonah, NY: Richard C. Owen.

Mudre, L. (2003) "Teaching versus Prompting: Supporting comprehension in guided reading" in *Developing Early Literacy: Report of the National Early Literacy Panel* (2008).

National Writing Project (2002) "Thinking About the Reading/Writing Connection with David Pearson" *The Voice*, 7:2.

Opitz, M. & Ford, M. (2001) *Reaching Readers: Flexible and innovative strategies for guided reading*. Portsmouth, NH: Heinemann.

Ogle, D. M. (1986) "K-W-L: A teaching model that develops active reading of expository text" *The Reading Teacher*, February, 39(6), 564–570.

O'Reilly, J. & Yau, M. (2009) *2008 Parent Census, Kindergarten-Grade 6: System overview and detailed findings*. Toronto, ON: Research and Information Services, Toronto District School Board.

Pearson, P. D. & Gallagher, M. C. (1983) "The Instruction of Reading Comprehension" *Contemporary Educational Psychology*, 8, 317–344.

Pinnell, G. & Scharer, P. (eds) (2003) *Teaching for Comprehension in Reading Grades K–2*. New York, NY: Scholastic Professional Books.

Raphael, T. & Au, K. (2006) *QAR Now: A powerful and practical framework that develops comprehension and higher-level thinking in all students*. New York, NY: Scholastic.

Rog, L. Jamison (2003) *Guided Reading Basics*. Markham, ON: Pembroke.

Smith, L. (1998) *Implementing the Reading-Writing Connection* at http://literacymethods.wikispaces.com/file/view/SCP98.8.pdf

Stead, T. (2006) *Reality Checks: Teaching reading comprehension with nonfiction K–5*. Portland, ME: Stenhouse.

Tierney, R. J. & Shanahan, T. (1996) "Research on the Reading-writing Relationship: Interactions, transactions, and outcomes" in R. Barr, M. L. Kamil, P. B. Mosenthal & P. D. Pearson (eds.), *Handbook of Reading Research: Volume II* (246–280). White Plains, NY: Longman.

Torgeson, J. et al. (2007) *Academic Literacy Instruction for Adolescents: A guidance document from the Center on Instruction*. Portsmouth, NH: RMC Research Corporation, Center on Instruction at www.centeroninstruction.org

Tovani, C. (2000) *I Read It But I Don't Get It*. Portland, ME: Stenhouse.

Tyner, B. (2004) *Small-group Reading Instruction: A differentiated teaching model for beginning and struggling readers*. Newark, DE: IRA.

Vaughn, J. L. & Estes, T. H. (1986) *Reading and Reasoning Beyond the Primary Grades*. Boston, MA: Allyn & Bacon.

Wise Brown, M. (1949) *The Important Book*. New York, NY: Harper-Collins.

Index